Some Will Be King Makers:

A Single Mother's Journey Raising African American Males

Deborah Watkins

𝓜2𝓜

Copyright © Deborah Watkins
Printed in USA by M2M Publishing

Editor: Karen Rogers
Cover Design: Tamyara Brown

Interior Layout: Kenisha Parker

All rights reserved. No part of this book may be reproduced or transmitted in any form or by any means without written permission from the author.

ISBN: 978-0-692-82613-3

M2M Publishing
P.O. Box 1122,
Buffalo, NY 14204

www.mediocre2marvelous.com

And the angel of the Lord said unto her, "Behold, thou art with child, and shall bear a son and shall call his name Ishmael; BECAUSE THE LORD HATH HEARD THY AFFLICTION."

Genesis 16:11

TABLE OF CONTENTS

Dedication

Acknowledgments

Foreword

Introduction

Chapter	1	Balanced not Perfect
Chapter	2	Change your Environment
Chapter	3	Strive for Stability
Chapter	4	Not smarter just exposed
Chapter	5	I am not a father
Chapter	6	We are not just body but we are also spirit
Chapter	7	Hoorah
Chapter	8	Grasshopper
Chapter	9	Those is some bad&^% kids
Chapter	10	Ignorance of the law is no excuse

Dedication

I dedicate this book to all the single mothers out there making it happen. This journey is not an easy one, but it is not impossible. I also dedicate this book to my two future Kings: Malcolm Louis and Marcus James.

Acknowledgement

I would like to thank those individuals who have supported me in this journey. My family and closest friends: Lenora Love and family, Darryl McAdory, Karen Moore, Darius Anderson, Pastor D'Mott.

My church family who have helped me raise these boys: My Bishop, Troy A. Bronner, Minister Shirley Goodwin, Pastor Tommy McClam, Pastor Herman Potts, Tim Hogue, Minister Renita Chadwick, Minister Dockery and the Boys to Men ministry.

I would like to thank the teaching staff at the Montessori school, especially Teddy, Shelia, the two Cheryls and Matt. I would like to thank the men of the community: Mr. Willis from Pratt Williard, Minister Kenny Simmons, Minister Frank Bostick, Squirt Redden, and Pappy Martin.

I would like to thank Dr. Marianne Sullivan who kept pushing me to put my book out there.

Foreword

Raising African American boys in today's society can be very difficult. Amidst all of the violence that is being reflected both through the media and in our own communities, the task of raising boys under these circumstances proves to be disheartening to say the least.

As an African American male who was raised by single women I can attest first hand to the struggles that the matriarchs around me had to face. This book captures the essence of the choices, changes, and challenges that being a single mother of African American boys may face in her quest to raise kings.

Raising kings in a culture where not many kings reign is what the author, in my opinion, has done an excellent job of conveying. Some would say, "It takes a king to raise a king." I beg to differ. In a generation where African American kings have abandoned their thrones or who have tried to reign, though they are still "princes" themselves, Queens have risen up, put on their crowns and taken up the scepter of responsibility to make sure that African American princes become African American kings.

When I was asked to review this work by Deborah Watkins, I was faced with the fact that I have not given birth to any sons of my own, yet I have been influential as a godfather, uncle, and spiritual father to many sons and from this position I was able to help to bring them to levels of maturity and success.

Peer pressure, societal pressure, and environmental pressure are just a few of the things that single mothers have to face as they raise their sons. Ms. Watkins has provided several principles from her own journey to assist other single mothers of African American boys to succeed as parents.

My hope and prayer for you is as you read through these pages, the principles such as being a balanced parent, providing a stable home and finding male role models for sons will be a force of light that will guide you on your journey of becoming a King Maker.

Bishop Dr. Troy Anthony Bronner, Elim Christian Fellowship, Buffalo, NY

Introduction

Common sense is an interesting concept. I consider myself hip, cool and having my hand on the pulse of what is happening out there, because I am open to new experiences, and because I have young children. I have come to realize that you do not need to be hip and cool, you just have to use common sense, and keep your hand on the pulse. I know that sounds too simple; however, I have dealt with too many parents who do not make good decisions about their lives and their children's lives.

I, like other parents, want my children to be successful, and realize that I am competing with many distractions. Because of where I work and through conversations with my clientele, I also realize how blessed I am to have had the parents I had, as imperfect as they were. They gave us a lot more than what our generation is giving their children. My parents had common sense. They did not have a lot of material things. They did not have a formal education. Nevertheless, what they gave me has carried me a lot further than my college degrees could ever carry me.

However, I have found that this common sense thing is not so common.

Working in the prison system is what I did for a living, having risen to the level of Deputy Superintendent of Programs. I worked in that system for 33 years on the rehabilitation side of prison under the title of corrections counselor for most of those 33 years. I ran therapeutic groups as well as one on one sessions with inmates. It was during those sessions that I learned a lot about the male psyche.

I was exposed to black males of multiple backgrounds and age groups. From my complete prison experience, particularly my counseling work, it became clear to me how one's childhood can affect the decisions they make later in life. Besides working in the prison, I am an artist, a friend, a lover, a Christian and a leader. I have performed in live shows was at one time a certified fitness instructor, and am now a writer to name a few of my professions. However, the most important thing I am is a mother.

I am a single mother of African American twin boys, who at this print are twenty-two years old. One is still in college, the other has graduated from college and is

Some Will Be King

working in a successful career. My singleness is not by choice; I would like to be married, but that is not how the cards fell for me. My boys have not had a relationship with their father by choice; he has decided not to be a father to them. Therefore, I had the awesome responsibility of raising them by myself. It is hard—Lord knows it is hard—but as the elders always say, "You made your bed, now you have to lie in it." So here I lie. However, I made up my mind that my bed was going to be firm, but comfortable. I was going to sleep on good sheets. Thus I took on motherhood with a definite strategy.

I know by the grace of God and good teaching that being a parent is the most important thing that I will ever do. I also know that you can only parent a person to a certain age; eventually they are going to be unleashed out into society. I decided that I wanted my boys to contribute to society in a good way. I want them to be Kings. I also knew that I wanted them to do what I have not done so far and that is not to live a routine life. Not that there is anything wrong with a routine life and if they chose to live one, that is okay, but I just want them to know that they have choices.

What am I going to unleash to society? I had to ask myself that question. I knew from working in the prison system, which is comprised of mostly African American males, that some individuals for whatever reason did not realize that the decisions they made as parents cost our society a lot of heartache.

Let me clarify and say that not every person who winds up in prison is the result of bad parenting; some came from good homes, but chose to go left. However, many of them came from a mess. Yes, I could hold on to the premise of white oppression and the end results of that. I agree that there is injustice in the criminal justice system, towards minorities; however, not everyone sitting in prison is innocent.

In fact, the majority are not innocent; they were just poorly represented. They should be doing some time but not as much. They should be restored, and then placed back in society. That may not happen. Therefore, because of that, we should be fighting even harder to change the mindset that leads to criminal behavior. It is very hard to return to society and be successful. Too many elements have to be in place to make it happen. Some have those support systems, some do not.

Criminal behavior is not a black thing. That was one of my biggest arguments with African American inmates during our counseling sessions. They used to talk as if all African Americans committed crimes, but just were not caught, and that I was an exception to the rule—that was why I did not wind up in prison. I would kindly inform them that African American prisoners only represent a small portion of the African American community. Most African Americans are law abiding, working class people.

According to the 2010 U. S. Census, the United States black population on April 1, 2010, was 42 million. Of that 42 million, 2.3 million are military veterans. More military veterans are black than any other minority group.

There were 2.5 million black college students in the fall of 2008. Of that 2.5 million an estimated 919,000 are African American males.

The Justice Policy Institute reported that in 2009 there were an estimated 827,680 African American males in prison and jail. That sounds like there are just as many men in prison as there are in college. However, if you look closer, the average age of a college student is between 18 and 24.

According to a study done by Iain Murray in a column for TechCentralStation.com, of the number of African American men 18-24, there were 480,000 in college and 180,000 in prison or jail. A young African American male is, in fact, two-and-a-half times as likely to be in college as prison or jail.

To sum it all up, less than 2% of African Americans engage in criminal behavior. However, I will in all fairness to the ones who are incarcerated, say this again, that the criminal justice system is unfair in how African Americans are sentenced and represented.

A report from the Urban league in 2007 showed that black men are nearly seven times more likely to be incarcerated, with average jail sentences about ten months longer than those of their white counterparts.

According to a testimony given by the Department of Justice before the United States Sentencing Commission, a survey of inmates in State and Federal Correctional facilities showed between 1994 and 2002, the average time served by African Americans for a drug offense increased by 73%, compared to an increase of 28% for white drug offenders. In addition, African Americans now serve virtually as much time in prison for a drug offense (57.2 months) as whites do for a violent offense (58.8 months). Therefore in that regard, yes, for the less than 2% percent who are caught up in the criminal justice system, some of you have been sold a bill of goods. However, there comes a point in time when one has to say to his- or herself, that I can control my own destiny up to a certain degree.

What degree? one may ask; we can control everything outside of accidents, natural disasters, terminal illnesses, or being the victim of a crime. Again, most African Americans are law-abiding working class people, but too few really live a life that is fulfilling and purposeful. Life for them has become mundane and predictable. It has become complicated over nothing. We create unnecessary drama out of boredom.

Parenting is largely about who you are, more so than a concrete guideline. I realize that the decisions I've made in terms of my children, were about how I perceived the world around me, how I felt about myself and the exposure I had in life.

Unfortunately, a single parent is raising more and more African American children. According to a study done by the National Council on Family Relations, from 1970 to 1988 the proportion of one-parent families among blacks increased from 33.0 to 55.6 %. A recent study from 2015 Census Bureau has shown that that number is now somewhere around 72%.

Black children are significantly more likely to live with their mothers only. Therefore, the reality is that many children are being raised in an unbalanced situation. Many people may disagree with the term that I use when I say unbalanced, but sometimes the truth is not pretty.

When I walk through some of the neighborhoods, I see young men with a look of sadness on their faces. When I ride the bus or train, I look at young men with no sense of pride in their appearance. I see young men trying to look like thugs and "gangstas" on hip hop videos, and I realize something: We do not raise our children to dream about doing extraordinary things. We do not teach our children to embrace uniqueness. We just raise our children. My pastor was preaching one Sunday and he stated that some of us were destined to be Kings/Queens, but some will be King Makers. I embraced that concept and made it my quest to make kings of my boys.

I find several different approaches when it comes to single parenting:

1. I am not in control, I am helpless, and do the best I can.
2. I am overprotective because I made mistakes and I do not want my child to make any.
3. I have to give them everything that I did not have, material-wise.
4. I have to overcompensate for the other parent not being there.
5. I am stuck with this child or these children and it is not fair so I am just going to go for mine. What about the children? Well, too bad; I cannot do everything.

Lastly, a very sad one:

6. I cannot do this; therefore, I am going to give them up.

Let us talk about the first approach:

1. ***I am not in control, I am helpless, and do the best I can.*** There is a true portion in that statement; we all probably try to do the best we can. However, the untruth in that statement is that you can be in control of your children, and you are not helpless. Unfortunately, we do not ask for the right help. Due to a number of things that happen to people in their lives, being a victim sometimes is an easy path to take. When you are a victim, you can blame someone else. Sometimes, due to rejection issues and the lack of knowledge, we do not keep seeking the help we need in the African American community. We cannot help our children because we cannot help ourselves.

2. ***I am overprotective, because I made mistakes and I do not want my children to make any.*** I am sorry to inform you of this but not only are your children going to make mistakes, but you are going to make some more mistakes as long as you are on this earth. However, and unfortunately for some of us, there was not a lot of tolerance for

mistakes. There was some severe backlash for mistakes. Some individuals were heavily scorned for mistakes, or made to feel some kind of inadequacy. In addition, there is a lot of judgment that goes on in our community. Mistakes, though, are how we learn actually, and people who are void of them have limited their growth and understanding about life.

3. *I have to give them everything that I did not have material-wise.* This one is really a hard one in the African American community, because we are so material driven. I am not saying that we should not want nice things. What I am saying is that we have an unhealthy attitude towards material things. We have things yet we still feel and act inadequate. We place way too much value on material things that have no value. Moreover, we place no value on the things that can take us out of our condition, e.g. education, exposure, and spirituality.

4. *I have to overcompensate for the other parent not being there.* I know the feeling, been there done

that. Well here is the hard truth: We can never compensate for the other parent. Unfortunately, if the other parent is not there, our child or children will have a void in their lives. It does not mean that they will be dysfunctional, or psychotic, or a failure. It just means that they will have to come to grips with it one day and that is where spirituality will have a major part in helping them keep it together.

5. *I am stuck with this child or these children and it is not fair, so I am just going to go for mine.* What about the children? Well too bad; I cannot do everything. I know raising children, as a single parent is hard; I will tell anyone it is hard. Do Not Do It! However, if circumstances or decisions dictate that you have to go it alone, you cannot take on the aforementioned attitude, because remember, you are unleashing someone onto society. Do you want that on your conscience that you unleashed a monster that may hurt other people or themselves? Perhaps you do not care, and if so, that is very sad and disquieting.

Some Will Be King

6. ***I cannot do this; therefore, I am going to give them up.*** Unfortunately, that may be the best choice; especially if your self-improvement is going to be a lengthy process. What I mean by that is some people are coming off drugs or some other traumatic situation, and it is going to take some time for them to get on the right track. The responsibility of raising a child is not a good thing for them right now; they just are not capable. Those cases always make me sad. There is nothing more horrible than a child being taken from their parents.

I became aware of these different mindsets, as I have interacted with other parents through various situations: i.e., church, school, sports, and social events. I also learned from the incarcerated parents I have talked to over the 30 years I worked in the prison system. I learned from other parents and I have advised other parents.

So what is the mindset and approach that we should have in raising our children, and does it apply to everyone? Nothing applies to everyone. I have just studied the families that I felt gave their children what they needed to be balanced and whole, and they all had some basics in common. I embraced those characteristics and it has been successful for me.

Here is the mindset I feel you should have: First, God has blessed me to have children. Children are not a burden they are a blessing, because they teach us about life. Raising my children can be a fun adventure. This is an enormous responsibility, but I am going to try to squeeze in fun every chance I get. There is so much out there that I can teach them and they can teach me and we will have fun doing it. Do you notice an underlying theme that is surfacing here? Yes, fun. Parenting should be and can be fun. It does not always have to be a struggle. Take your mind off the struggle sometimes and try to find the beauty in your child. If it is not fun, make it fun. I am telling you it will get you through a lot of sleepless nights. Again, it's the mindset.

Once you become a parent it is no longer about you, but that does not mean you cannot enjoy it. All it means is that you have to change your lifestyle. This needs to be defined, because some of us do not understand that parenting is a lifestyle just like anything else. We will explore this concept. Everything I present in this book will be about raising black males. I am focusing on boys because that is what I know. In addition, African American boys are becoming an endangered species and we need to talk about it and stop putting our heads in the sand about it.

This is a guide; it is not the only way, the truth and the light. My hope is that through my experiences I will be able to shed some light on parenting as a single mom. There are some key elements I feel have to be in place in order to be successful at parenting an African American boy. These elements can and will motivate them into wanting to live an extraordinary life. You will be releasing Kings out into the world and not Killers.

1. They have to have a balanced parent.
2. They have to live in a certain environment.
3. They have to have a stable home.
4. They have to have exposure to different things.
5. They have to have male role models.
6. They have to have a spiritual base.
7. They have to have cheerleaders.
8. They have to have a mentor for their gifts.
9. They have to have discipline.

10. They need to be taught about the criminal justice system.

We will explore each of these topics in subsequent chapters. This is a workbook. There will be questions and exercises after each chapter. Work through the questions; they will help you better understand yourself and your children.

Chapter 1

Balanced not perfect

I was 33 years old, college educated, had a steady job, and was a homeowner; all I needed was a husband and some kids and then I would have the perfect life. My friends were getting married, and I was becoming impatient. I began to make very unwise decisions in my relationships because I wanted so desperately to have what I saw was the perfect life. I was in an uncommitted relationship. I knew, but I was willing to compromise myself. I got tired of waiting for Mr. Right, and became pregnant. So when I discovered that I was having his children (twins) and he seemed supportive, I, as many women before me, thought that this would solidify our relationship. We broke up before they were born. My life has not been perfect.

I could feel myself spiraling emotionally and knew that if I did not pull it together, it would not be good for my children or me. It was stressful having two babies to care for at the same time. However, the voice inside kept telling me you can do this; you are going to be all right. I analyzed my situation and I knew this, that:

1. I had to stay employed.
2. I had to maintain a home.
3. I had to have transportation.
4. I had to have childcare.
5. I had to keep dreaming.

Remaining employed was not very difficult, because I had been working at my job for a number of years, and was secure. All I had to do was show up and I was pretty much home free, so I thought. I was doing this alone and had already used up all of my sick time.

I wound up home for nine months living on half pay due to complications with the pregnancy. When I returned to work after having the children, I had no sick time or vacation time left. It was stressful because I knew that I had to stay employed.

My parents were supportive emotionally, and they really wanted to help physically, but they were both ill and just could not do it. I had put myself in a bad position, but I could not give up.

Their father had his own problems and could not handle any more responsibility, so he was no support. I came to work sick or well; I was trying to keep up a good front and I did, but inside I could feel myself crumbling. My best friend was there for me, as most women are there for each other. I had been there for her during her crisis and she never forgot it.

It was an isolated life for a while, because I had two small babies, and that limits the places you can go, especially by yourself. Nevertheless, I got out, especially in warm weather, I would get out. I would walk around the park. I would go to outdoor events. I would go to the mall. It helped my frame of mind. The fresh air knocked the children out and they would sleep well at night. That helped me to stay healthy enough mentally, so I could keep my job. It was not easy. I would be lying if I said it was, but I had to persevere.

Maintaining a home was a challenge because I had just bought my home, had not been it for over one year, and there are many hidden expenses with home ownership.

Children are very expensive and budgeting was something that I had to pay attention to for the first time in my life. Budgeting was not my strong point—it still is not—but I have never let myself get too out there.

I had my share of debt, I still do, but I was determined to stay in my home and I did. I always tell people if at all possible stay in your home. If there has to be a choice between paying your rent or mortgage and paying a bill, pay the rent or mortgage, because you can think your way out of a situation if you have a place to lay your head.

If you do not have shelter, you cannot even think your way out of a situation. If you do not have lights, you can always buy candles. If you do not have heat, you can go for help to get heat. If you do not have any food, you can always go to a shelter, a soup kitchen, church, or relative to get food. However, it is more difficult to get a place to stay, especially when you have children.

I had a car, but I also had a car note. If I had been wise, I would have kept the car I had because it was almost paid for and in good working condition. I made an unwise decision to trade it in for a bigger car. That was a very unwise decision. However, since I had made the decision and I needed a car to get to work, again, I had to keep it and keep it running.

Childcare was a very serious issue for me. Both my parents were elderly, and in poor health and were not able to help with the kids. Childcare expenses can make you or break you and it was breaking me. It was not easy. I depended on the kindness of one of my church members who had a day care. She only charged me for the one child. It was still expensive.

You have to keep looking until you can find affordable, safe childcare. When you find it, do not take advantage of the people who are helping you out. People take advantage of their daycare providers. They will not pay them on time. They will not pick up their children on time. Therefore, they wind up having to leave one daycare provider after another. They find themselves in a situation where they do not have childcare, and they cannot come to work.

You cannot take advantage of people and expect them to take it. I never had that problem. I had to sacrifice the things that I wanted, but I paid my childcare provider. We are still friends to this day; when I could help her out I did. We took care of each other.

One of the best things I did for myself at this crucial time was join a good bible teaching church. Worshipping, reading and studying the word helped me with my emotions. It was imperative that I get my emotions in check. Emotions gone unchecked make us eat too much, shop too much, drink too much, smoke too much and choose wrong relationships. I am not just referring to male/female relationships, but all relationships. I had to make some crucial decisions. I was no longer single without children. I had to change my lifestyle.

My life was not perfect; I had to make some major adjustments. However, in spite of all I had to face, my life was in balance. It was in balance because I had grown up. I was no longer in Kansas. I also was no longer in Oz. I was in reality and I had to face it. It was a reality that I created. I now know that there were some unseen spiritual forces working against me, because I was in a Bible teaching church. I learned a lot; I was willing to learn and that was to my benefit. It was to my benefit because you have to be teachable in life. No one has all the answers. If we had all the answers, we would not be in some of the circumstances that we wound up in.

You are probably asking yourself, how was her life in balance? It sounded like a mess. Balance is not about being perfect. It is not about always making good decisions. It is about how you handle life. Life is going to happen, but how you deal with it is what counts.

Being in balance is the ability to look at your situation, analyze the facts, determine what your options are, and make the best decision at the time. Balance is not making decisions based on emotions. I had to change my lifestyle. I did not like it; I will be the first to admit to that; however, I had to accept it. I had to come up with new options for myself.

I had built some very strong friendships with people over the years, and fortunately for me, what I built was there for me when I needed it. They are like family to me. These people were willing to pitch in and help me. Why, I do not know ... maybe because I had pitched in and helped them when they were down or needed help. Maybe it was just God's favor.

I honestly do not know why people were so willing to help me. I do know that I was not too proud to say I needed help, and I did not take advantage when people were willing to help me. The Bible talks about how you make friends. It states that you must first show yourself friendly. That principle worked for me because I was able to call on friends, instead of family when I needed help. Again, I did not take advantage of the friendship. Whenever I went too far out there, they would reel me back in.

That is balance; you do not take people for granted. You try to give more than you take. You learn how to sacrifice. I was never late picking my children up from daycare. I always paid sitters on time, what I owed, and if I was going to be late, which was hardly ever, I let them know in advance. I never behaved as if I was doing them a favor by letting them watch my children; I let them know that I was grateful and I showed it.

Some Will Be King

Excess times ten. Americans, we are excess driven, and we can never get enough. However, when you are balanced, you realize that, that is not a healthy attitude, even if you earn a lot of money. There are people who belong to a common club: they make a lot of money, but have never made good investments, or thought about how to share what they have. Some of these people wind up in bankruptcy court. Some of these people commit suicide. They were not living balanced. When is there enough of anything?

There are many of us black women who are putting ourselves in financial ruin, because we are always trying to live copycat lives. We see someone is wearing a certain style, or the latest trend; even though we cannot afford to, we want to run out and buy it. We feel that those things give us our value, make us popular or will make us happy, only to find out that they are just a waste of your money.

I have met many women who look good, dressed to the nines; however, they had the same insecurities as I had when we sat down and had a heart-to-heart talk. They are driving the latest vehicle, but their children are flunking out of school. How does your son flunk out of school and you are driving a Mercedes?

Instant gratification. We live in a society now where waiting is not popular. When you are balanced, you understand that sometimes you have to wait. There usually is good reason why you should wait. It gives you time to think of alternatives. Most times when you wait, whatever it was that had you so in wanting loses its appeal after a while anyway.

I know people who cannot wait for anything, so they beg, borrow and steal to get what they want at that time. These people are always struggling, always. They borrow so much that people start to avoid them. They lose friends, because they do not pay them back. A balanced person tries to make it a habit not to borrow from other people.

If it is not life or death, it is a good habit not to borrow money from friends and family. I have seen family members not speaking to each other for years because of someone borrowing money and then not paying it back. When you are not living balanced, you become consumed by whatever your focus is and you start to neglect other areas. Your children may become victims of your neglect.

Money and material things are not the only things that cause us to become unbalanced. Some people are caught up in activities, busy work. This boils down to what are your priorities. I will tell anyone, if you are a parent, your children are your first priority.

There was a time when I first became born again, that I was in church just about every day. I thought that, that was what a good Christian should do. Especially one like me who had so many sins to atone for (smile). It was my safe haven from having to face certain realities.

Some religions operate out of guilt so we feel many times that we have to be doing something in the church. I tried to do things that would show everyone that I was a good Christian. The reality is unless you work for the church for a living, there is no reason for you to be there every day. There is no reason to be anywhere other than your home every day, not even your job.

Some people work every single day. Even the Lord, according to the Bible, rested on the seventh day. If for financial reasons you have to work every day, it should only be temporary. You should be strategizing how you can live on less money until you can obtain a higher paying job.

Go to free financial workshops on how to balance your budget. Go to the library, read books on how to handle your money. Take your children with you to the library. Find out about all the freebees in the community. The newspaper, community papers, community center bulletin boards, and library bulletin boards are a good source to find out about free things in your community.

Go to those events and take your children with you; they will love you for it. If you need to make more money, then you need to do some research on what jobs are paying more, and get a plan on how to obtain the skills needed for that job. I worked a job that was not the most pleasant place to work and probably dangerous to some. It was a government job; therefore, it was stable and it had benefits. You may have to do some things that you do not like, but if it has benefits, you had better grin and bear it and thank God that you have health benefits for your children.

Finally, you can become unbalanced when it comes to people. As human beings, we want to be connected to other human beings. I always say to God, "you know this is a cruel joke, to make us need and want other human beings."

No matter how much we say we do not care and we do not need anybody, we do.

Even if you are a super saint and you are always in prayer and reading the Bible 24 hours a day, when you pull your head up from that Bible, you still want to be connected to someone here on earth. That is bittersweet, and where the danger lies. Because when we become involved with others, our emotions come into play. Either we like them or we dislike them. We either love them or hate them. These are emotions, which can be very tricky and deceitful. This is why being true to you and loving who that self is, is so important. What does that mean? Very simple, do not let anyone tell you what is good for you.

Seek your own truth about what is real and good for you. That can only come from the spirit inside. Nothing on the outside should ever define you. I find that most people really do not have a mind of their own. We are always trying to talk like someone else, dress like someone else, walk like someone else, go where someone else goes, style our hair like someone else's. We do this sometimes no matter how silly it looks.

It is one thing for children to mimic the behavior of others; after all, they are impressionable. It is embarrassing; however, to watch grown up people do this to themselves; it really is. Sometimes we are hanging with a crowd that we think is the in crowd. We don't feel good about how they treat us at times, but we still hang. Most importantly, you are sending the wrong message to your children. Try to instill in them that whatever that special gift is that is inside of them, it is good enough. Teach them that who they are is good enough.

So many of us do not feel that who we are, or what we have inside of us, is good enough. Therefore, we compare ourselves to others. I had to get over that type of thinking; so I am being honest in saying that I had to come to that conclusion myself also.

We need to tell our boys that they do not have to try to be like anyone else because, baby boy, you are wonderful the way God made you. You cannot do this; however, if you do not spend a lot of time with your children. How else will you know what that special gift is, if you do not spend time with them?

Some Will Be King

Find out what your special gift is, then you can appreciate what your baby boys' specialness is. Spending a lot of time with your family is what balance is. I never stop dreaming. Our dreams give us hope, purpose, and a reason to get up in the morning. We should always be working to become balanced not perfect.

Questions:

1. What is your interpretation of the statement balanced not perfect?
2. How does this apply to your life at the present time?
3. How do you think your children view their world based on how they see you handle life?
4. Are you living within your means?
5. What steps have you taken to better your situation if needed?

Exercise:

Take your child(ren) to a free community event. Ask them how they felt about it. What did they dislike or like about it? What did you learn about your children's interests as a result?

Chapter 2

Change your Environment

This chapter only applies to you if you live in the wrong neighborhood. What is the wrong neighborhood? A neighborhood that is distracting and dangerous. African American boys are going to seek male role models. They are going to look for identity. Unfortunately, single moms, we are not their identity. People were always telling me, Deborah you are doing such a good job with your boys. You have such good boys. You are a good mother. I would always look at them strangely, because I did not feel that I was doing anything any different from anyone else. I still do not feel that I am doing something special.

I do know that I am blessed, that when I had them, some key elements were in place. One of those elements is that I lived in a neighborhood where I was not competing with gang members, criminals, the dope man and a whole lot of social ills for my children's attention. I was also a homeowner. That right there made my life less stressful.

Some Will Be King

I live right in the inner city. I live in a quiet neighborhood that hardly has any children. It did not dawn on me at first that this was a good thing. I wanted them to have neighborhood friends, as I had when I was growing up. In retrospect, it probably was a good thing that they did not have neighborhood friends, because neighbors today are not like the ones I had growing up. Unfortunately, you do not know what people are doing behind closed doors. There is unhealthy activity going on even in the best of neighborhoods.

One day could ruin your child's life forever. Therefore, I was fortunate not to have to compete with neighborhood children and their families. Where I live is affordable and decent. I never had to consider living in the suburbs. The suburbs in Buffalo, NY did not appeal to me because I do not feel African Americans are embraced in most suburbs, and therefore, they never appealed to me.

I never wanted to live in a predominantly white neighborhood, or white suburb as an adult, even though I lived in a predominantly white neighborhood as a child. I am not knocking anyone if they are. I just know that it can be just as stressful living in a predominately white neighborhood with black children, as it can be living in a gang infested, drug dealing neighborhood. It just becomes a different kind of stress. Stress is stress.

I have had many conversations with black parents living in predominantly white neighborhoods and most of them say that it was not what they thought it would be. They expressed that they were constantly battling with the teachers in the suburban schools, just as they were battling in the inner city public schools. However, now they are paying higher taxes to battle. What they encountered was as their boys starting getting older and bigger, the attitudes toward them changed. Once their boys were of driving age, they would constantly be pulled over by the local police.

Police who should have known, and most times did know, who they were. Most said if they could live in a black suburb, that would be their first choice. How they were able to survive a lot of the nonsense, was due to the fact that there were two parents in the home. Having that strong father figure, helped them through a lot of the drama. A single mom would probably not get the same respect. Having done some research on this issue, I found that this was not unique to just Buffalo, NY.

I found an article in the Detroit News, written by Cindy Rodriguez, October 2007, the topic <u>Many Metro Blacks feel isolated in suburbs.</u> In the article an African American doctor moved to the suburbs of Detroit, MI. He realized that he could get more for his money, in terms of safety, auto insurance, money spent for private schools, and property taxes, by moving there. However, life in the predominantly white suburb was hard on them in other ways: They felt isolated (there was only one other black family in their neighborhood), their children were ostracized in middle school, and they felt making connections with other African Americans meant trekking to Detroit on the weekends.

In another article from the web site <u>The Authentic Voice,</u> Elizabeth Liorente, writes about a family from Paterson, N.J. who moved to Ridgewood, a suburb. They stated that it seemed like a picture perfect life, until the family's daughter came home from her first week of school in tears. The only black girl in her first-grade class, she told her mother that none of the children would hold her hand when they stood in a circle. A girl standing beside her in class recoiled and blurted: "Your color might rub off on me."

In another article from the Milwaukee Journal Sentinel, written by Felicia Thomas-Lynn Feb. 25, 2003, there are stories about the strides of African Americans being able to move to the suburbs of Milwaukee, but some families said they made conscious decisions to remain in the city.

One mother stated in the article that "The suburbs simply aren't friendly. I didn't want my children affected by some of the unspoken messages that I receive when I shop in the suburbs," she said. "People who live in the suburbs ascribe to you all the negative behaviors and stereotypical characterizations of African Americans that they see on television or read in the newspaper. Why put yourself through that?"

In "Growing up in the Suburbs 3-part series," Duane Lawton talks about his experiences as an African American male growing up in a Northern VA suburb. Lawton states in the article that scrutiny can be discreet, but often it's blatant. "It's as if residents (including some of the black ones) are just waiting to call the police on you and the police are just too eager to relentlessly patrol the neighborhood, (in vehicles, on foot and on bicycles) waiting for you to do something like *walk* just so they can stop you, search you and put you in handcuffs. This has happened to me, my brothers and my friends several times within the same day!" These are just a few of the many stories I found about black life in the suburbs.

I am not against anyone living in the suburbs; of course it is your choice and it could be a very good choice for you and your children. I just do not want people to be naïve about what could happen, and suggest you do your homework before moving into a situation like that. Find out if there are other African Americans living there and ask them about it. I think you will be surprised what you find out.

So I realized that I had a pretty good situation where I lived, a black neighborhood; it also comprised mostly homeowners who cared about the neighborhood and kept up their property. There were some rogues, but they were in the minority. In our case the few bad apples did not spoil the whole barrel. African American boys need to see African Americans living well.

Some Will Be King

My boys' exposure in the neighborhood was good. Once they were old enough they started going to a community center around the corner from where we lived after school. That gave me time to get home from work and gave them healthy recreation. They would play basketball there all day and many other activities. The older gentleman that ran the center was like a father to them and we will be eternally grateful to Mr. Willis for his concern. They were safe; he did not allow any violent behavior and the neighborhood supported that. This is an all African American neighborhood. They exist; you have to look for them. Do it before your children are school age and impressionable. Because there were not a lot of children on our street, I could better control whom they met.

My children like their home; they feel safe. The elementary school they attended was only one block away, truly a blessing. At age ten they would get themselves up for school, get themselves dressed, eat breakfast and walk to school. They crossed a huge major street. Raising them to be street smart, and with God's angels looking after them, I never had a problem. They were very cautious and

I knew to incorporate some of our neighbors. I informed some of my neighbors, that they were walking to school by themselves in the morning and asked that if they sensed trouble, would it be okay for them to knock on their door. My next-door neighbors, an elderly couple would look out for them. The community wants to help you most of the time. The elderly are our gift to society especially our African American elderly. If they see that you are trying to do the right thing with your life, they will become your biggest allies. My elderly neighbors were always looking out for the boys and me.

So what do you do if you do not have this type of neighborhood? You ask for help. You ask everyone you come in contact with, where is a good affordable neighborhood? We perish most of the time because of lack of knowledge. We don't stay focused. We don't set priorities. You go on a search for neighborhoods. Ask someone to take you around if you do not have a car. Offer them gas money of course, remember be balanced. Get a map, and hop on the bus.

I realize that there are people who fall into the categories of the poor and the working poor. They simply cannot afford to move to a better neighborhood. This is where you have to start thinking outside of the box. I often think about what I would do if I could not afford to live in a better neighborhood on my own.

A situation comedy that came on TV around the '80s, was about two single white women with children, who could not afford to live the lifestyle they wanted to live on their own. They moved into a house together with their children. I know that it is a cliché, but it is also truth: where there is a will there is a way. There is always more than one way. Section 8 will pay for housing in some suburban neighborhoods.

Some Will Be King

Some Will Be King

Make finding a good neighborhood your priority. You want your children to like being at home. They will like being at home, because *you* like being at home. I believe you have more influence over your home than you give yourself credit for. You create your own atmosphere. My boys like their home, and like being home, because they feel affirmed and loved.

If your children like being home, you are not competing with the world. I discovered early on that one of my boys was very social and musical. I discovered that the other one was more cerebral, not too social; he preferred one on one. I had to create an environment that catered to both their needs. It was challenging, but it has brought me so much joy and peace of mind.

They also are free to be who they are. I do not try to control or manipulate who they are. I try not to be too critical, when they make mistakes. We talk more about solutions, than who is to blame. Therefore, they very rarely make big mistakes. We laugh a lot in our home. We have clean parties with people who love us. They love to entertain; they love to have friends stay over. I taught them early on that our home was a community. Therefore, everyone has a part to play in the upkeep of this community.

By the time my boys were seven or eight years old, they were washing dishes, cleaning their rooms, taking out the garbage, and vacuuming the floors. By nine or ten, they were mopping floors and cleaning the bathroom. By eleven or twelve, they were cutting grass, and washing and drying their own clothes.

Therefore, when they turned thirteen, fourteen and fifteen it was a part of our lives and I did not have to fight with them to do something that they should be doing. They may have argued with me, but they did it. They also took

Some Will Be King

ownership of having a nice place to live. When they turned fifteen, they both painted their own rooms. I helped, but they did the majority of the work. They picked out their own colors. Did they do it perfectly? No, I was not looking for perfection, just teaching them responsibility.

Whenever I went out of town and I had someone stay with them, they would always say to me, "Girl, these boys are so self sufficient." I was proud of them. I knew people who could not leave their children with even family members because the children were too much of a burden. I always taught my boys, be an asset not a liability; always bring something to the table. I emphasized to them, if you see someone doing something, don't just stand there like a lump on a log, ask if you can help. They usually do, and people are so impressed with them.

Make finding a good neighborhood your priority. It will definitely pay off. Contact your neighborhood politicians for help; that's why we put them in office. Talk to your pastor. Remember the squeaky wheel gets the oil. Make a pest of yourself. You cannot care what people think when you are fighting for your children. Change your environment; remember, a home makes a neighborhood, so if they take ownership of their home, they will take ownership of their neighborhood. I hope that they will take ownership for society.

Questions:

1. If you are not in the neighborhood of your choice, what neighborhood would you choose?
2. Are you and your children safe in your home?
3. Do you know your local politicians?
4. Are you a member of a community organization?

Exercise:

Contact your local community leader and find out what services are available to you and your children.

Chapter 3

Strive for Stability

I have lived in a stable home pretty much all my life. My parents only lived in maybe four neighborhoods their entire lives in the city where I grew up. I see the value in that. I did not have to think about where I was going to live as a child. I pretty much lived a child's life. There are children out there that have to worry about where they are going to live. That is a burden they should not have to bear. They worry about where they are going to live because their parents are unstable. I am not talking about people with mental illness. I am talking about people who refuse to grow up and face their responsibilities.

How does this affect a child growing up with this type of parent? They can become distrustful of adults. They can become insecure. They will oftentimes feel that the person they are connected to is out of control, so they have to be the adult. They carry a certain amount of shame. Children are very sensitive; if you are not in control, they feel it.

There were times; however, when I was growing up, that our stability was tested. There was domestic violence in my home when I was a child. My mother would leave or my father would leave. I remember those were terrible times. As time went on and they matured in their marriage, it was not always a bowl of cherries, but for the most part they were pretty much settled. I could count on them being there. Even when their health was failing as they were aging, I could still count on them being there.

My mother was a homebody. I believe that if she had been a single parent she probably still would have been stable in terms of where she lived, because she was very responsible. I took after her in that sense; I have only lived in three places as an adult. Two of the three places I rented, and the one I own. My mother paid the bills for our family; she did not believe in not paying your bills. We were never homeless and we never did without the basics: food, shelter, and clothing. As an adult I have never been homeless or been evicted.

In the Webster's dictionary, the word "stable" comes from a Latin word "stabulum" meaning to put, keep, or live in, as in a stable where animals are kept. It also means capable of standing, firmly established, fixed, steadfast, not changing or fluctuating, steady in purpose, constant, and finally, able to resist alteration in chemical, physical, or biological properties.

I like the definitions for the word stable, because they support my belief. I like the definition, "steady in purpose." My dream for my boys is that they will someday find their true purpose and be able to operate in it. I knew early on that I had to have a stable environment for them. It gave them harmony in their thinking and their feelings. When the world was trying to beat them down, they always knew they had a place to lay their heads.

With a good night's sleep, tomorrow somehow does not look so bad. We have our challenges as all families do. They have their sibling squabbles like all families do. We have sickness, death, financial problems and life issues. However, where they live is home and it is a haven. It is one thing to live in a house, but it is another thing to have a home.

My children and I travel a lot. My children have gone off to overnight camps. They have gone to sleepovers. My one son, Malcolm is a homebody. He is not very social.

Therefore, when he feels overwhelmed, he wants to go home. I have been fortunate in that they have only lived in one house. I thank God. My son often says when we are away from home that he misses his house. He has said on many occasions, "I want to sleep in my own bed." That gave me a good feeling in my heart to know that my child feels comfort in his own bed. The fact that he is not worrying about that bed being snatched from under him is wonderful.

I can only imagine that my other son, Marcus feels the same way also. I never heard him verbalize it, but he always seems to be very happy at home. He is the musical one. The basement is his domain. There is a set of drums down there, a keyboard and guitars. I have had live concerts in my house. When my goddaughter would come over, she would play the keyboard When a boy from his school came over, he would play the guitar. Marcus would play the drums. My children feel comfortable enough to be silly and goofy. We sing, we dance, we laugh, we cry; it is home. There is a set of free weights in the basement. They have a place to study for their exams at school. Both of them usually receive merit role to honor roll grades in school.

I remember one night my boys went to a party at one of their schoolmate's house who lived around the corner from where we lived. After the party, they came home with company, two boys. Both of the boys they brought home were from their school, they were all 14 years old at the time. It was kind of late in the evening. The one boy lived three blocks away. I knew him; I had met his mom, and he had spent the night at our house before. I will refer to him as the "neighborhood boy." My boys had spent the night with him at his house before. He was a decent kid so I had no problems with him. The other boy I did not know. I did not know his mother or father. I did not know where he lived. I had never seen the boy a day in my life until that night. I will refer to him as the "stranger."

They asked me if the "stranger" could spend the night. I told them, "absolutely not." First, they did not ask me ahead of time. Second, what would be the reason for him spending the night? They just came from a party, there was no need for a sleepover, enough was enough. I asked them why couldn't he go home. They were hemming and hawing and I knew something was suspicious.

They finally gave a half-behind confession about the "stranger" coming to the party they had just come from with another child and his parent. He did not go home with the person he came with, because he thought he would be spending the night with the "neighborhood boy" who was now also at my house.

The "neighborhood boy's" mother told him when they walked to his house after the party, that the "stranger" could not spend the night at their house. Her reason she was having a sleepover for his little sister and there would be a lot of girls in the house. Her husband did not want a strange boy in the house. Therefore, "neighborhood boy" found himself in a heck of a predicament because it was late at night. My boys had walked to "neighborhood boy's" house with them and witnessed the whole situation. Not only would "neighborhood boy's" mother not let the boy spend the night, she also would not take him home.

I asked "neighborhood boy" why he did not make sure this boy could spend the night before, "stranger boy," missed his ride home. "Neighborhood boy" claimed he asked his mother beforehand while they were at the party over the phone, and that she must not have understood what he said. He claimed she told him that the boy could spend the night. I was really perturbed by the whole incident, so I called his mother and asked her side of the story. She told me he did not ask her and that the "stranger" could not spend the night at her house. I asked her would she take the boy home. She said no. I was now further perturbed with her response because it was her son's fault that the boy was now stranded. I was starting to believe her son, more so than her.

So now I have a strange kid in my house. A kid that my boys felt obligated to house and protect. They knew that their home was a safe haven. My children are usually good judges of character, so I was not concerned that he would murder us in our sleep. I analyzed the situation, because that is what balanced people do. I had three choices I felt: let him spend the night, put him out on the street, or call the police. I asked the "stranger" if I could talk to his mother.

He told an outlandish lie about his mother being out of town and there was no one home. I did not believe his story and could tell he was hiding something. Therefore, I threatened to call the police. I then let the four of them go down in the basement and stew over what I proposed.

They put their heads together and decided they had better tell me the whole truth. With crocodile tears, the "stranger" expressed to me that the truth of the matter was that his mother was home. He knew she would be angry at the fact that he missed a ride home, and he was more or less stranded. He knew that she would go off, because he could have been home instead of wandering the streets. He knew if he called her and she had to come and get him after she had arranged for his transportation to and from the party, it was not going to be pleasant, and he did not want to face her. I asked him why he told a lie; he said he was scared. I told him I did not like liars and because of that, he would never be able to spend the night at my house again.

This boy had told an outlandish lie about his mother's whereabouts. My boys had that puppy dog look in their eyes like, Mom, please do not put him out; they wanted him to be safe. They also did not want me to call the police. My instinct told me it was okay to let him stay. Besides, I did not feel like driving him home.

As I lay in my bed, after they all retreated to the basement, I asked myself how this all became my responsibility. I was perturbed with the "neighborhood boy's" mother who refused to let the kid in her home or take him home. After all, her son made the arrangements.

The next morning I told the two boys who had spent the night they had to go. I felt I had done my duty; I gave him a safe haven for the night. It was now daylight and he did not have to go home but he had to get the he%* out of here. I told the "neighborhood boy" whose mom would not take the stranger in, to take him home with him and ask his mother to take the boy home. I felt she could at least do that; after all, I housed him.

After a few minutes, and some hushed conversation, I heard the door shut. I looked out my bedroom window that faced the street, and I saw the two boys walking in the opposite direction of the "neighborhood boy's" house. I asked my boys where they were going. They told me the "neighborhood boy" was walking the "stranger" to the subway train. The four of them had scraped their pennies together to put the kid on the subway to go home. The "neighborhood boy" was still afraid to take the kid home with him, even after a good night's sleep. I analyzed this whole situation and I had to thank the Almighty.

There were some important factors here: Number one, my children knew that our home was a safe haven and they would rather face me, knowing that I would be upset, than to be unsafe. Two, they knew they could talk to me about it. The neighborhood kid who had two parents at home did not feel he could communicate with either one of them. He would not take the kid home with him. He would not ask his mother or his father to take the kid home.

Finally, three: the stranger boy did not feel he could call on his mother in a time of crisis; that was really sad to me. No matter how bad it gets, your children should feel like they can call on you no matter what time it is. I remember calling my father after midnight, after a concert one night when I was a teenager. My friends and I were stranded and he came and got us. He was not a happy camper, but I knew I could call on him. I also know that as mad as he was he was probably glad I called him.

Let's retreat back to another definition of the word stable that I like. That definition of the word stable is to be steadfast, able to resist alteration in chemical, physical, and biological properties. If you have stability in the home, you have no desire to escape from reality because reality is pretty good, not perfect but stable—balanced. You are better able to resist the temptations of the world because your world has been constant. You will not be so easily swayed. If you do not have stability, strive for it. When my boys turned 17, I was able to leave them for weeks at a time and they conducted themselves very responsibly.

Very Important! Do not allow violence in your home. What do I mean by violence? Violence is hitting, punching, kicking, threats, severe name-calling where someone is being brutalized. Do not have anyone in your home that is disrespecting you or your children. Your boys will resent you for it. It will make them angry towards women and angry towards the world. I never had anyone living with me. That is how I chose to live my life. I am not trying to preach to people how they should live theirs.

However, I will say that if you are going to have someone living with you, demand respect. Please do not subject your male children to violence especially. I work with men who have been very violent towards their community and society. It started at home. They told me stories of how their father used to beat their mother, or their mother's boyfriend was brutalizing everyone in the house. A lot of men do not respect women for that very reason. This is very critical to your son's emotional development. You are setting the standard for how your son will be as a man, a mate, a member of society.

Your house should be a home, a safe haven, a place of comfort, a place where people are celebrated, and feel loved. Strive for stability.

Questions:

1. How many places have you lived in the last five years?
2. Are your children afraid to bring anyone home with them? If so, why?
3. Is your home a sanctuary or a place to live? What does that statement mean to you?

Exercise:

Have your children write about an event that they had at their house. How did it make them feel?

Chapter 4

Not smarter just exposed

What gives children of other ethnicities the advantage over our children? Are children of other ethnicities smarter? Is it due to genetics ... is there something in our DNA? The answer is very simple, exposure.

I am perplexed as to why we place ourselves in a box in some African American communities. What puzzles me the most out of all the things that I observed about some African American parents during my travels, was our lack of interest in giving our children diverse exposure experiences. If you ask the experts, they want to blame it on a number of things: post-traumatic slave syndrome, conspiracies, and oppression. My question is this: If we are all descendants of slaves, why does one group of slave descendants think one way and the other descendants think another way? Is it because we are individuals who have the power to choose, or are we doomed to stay in a certain status? I don't know the answer, but what I do know is that how you are educated makes a difference.

Some of us have a definition of what is Black, and what is not, which leads to our attitudes about experiencing the unknown. I remember when my children were very young. I had family memberships to everything I could afford, the zoo, the science museum, the art museum, and the aquarium. One of the reasons for the memberships was that it gave us unlimited access to these places, and I like that access. It also was an inexpensive way to entertain my children, and educate them at the same time. We always had some place to go, because these places all had "members only" events. Wait a minute ... did I say educate my children? Did I mean that I am also responsible for my children learning new things and not just school? If you did not know, you are their first teacher.

Besides access, memberships to these places gave us certain privileges. People who were not members never knew about the many other features at some of these places. For example we were allowed to go to the back of the tanks at the aquarium to see how they set up displays.

Some Will Be King

At the zoo there were special classes where the children could hold certain animals.

I noticed something, though—and it started to disturb me—whenever my children and I would be at a member-sponsored event, you could count on two hands the number of African Americans that would be there. The staff at these places would look at us somewhat strangely. They would be indifferent, because they were not used to black people being members.

My children would bring it to my attention—children are not as naïve as we think. They asked me, "How come we are always the only black people here?" I found that I had no answer, because Buffalo, NY has a decent size African American population. I pondered that question. I found that I still had no answer. I began to question my own motives. Was I identifying with something outside of my true self? Was I living in an unrealistic world? Because I honestly felt and believed that we had as much right to be at these events as any other family regardless of our race.

Some Will Be King

Children's Museum in Pennsylvania

Grand Canyon

Some Will Be King

Some Will Be King

I was interested in learning still and I saw no harm. I concluded that we did have the right, and nothing was wrong with me. I also felt, why can't I, as an African American, be interested in different things? Why does being curious about life translate to being white? However, because so few of us participated in these memberships, we would get strange looks from the staff of these places whenever we showed up.

 I remember taking my boys to a Saturday morning science class at the science museum; the woman teaching the class was just downright rude. Therefore, the rebellious side of me would go to every class, even if I did not want to, just because of her attitude. Then I would bring other children along also.

 Whenever I would tell other African American mothers where I was going with my children, they either showed no interest, or talked as if they didn't have time. Therefore, for a long time my boys and I were lone rangers. I do not regret it one bit. Whenever we went to another city or another state, we would go to museums there.

 Many times having a membership to the science museum and zoo in our hometown also gave us access to the science museum and zoos in another town free of charge. It was a benefit. Some of you are probably thinking, I can't afford all of these memberships. Not true. A membership for a family usually costs less than those $100.00 sneakers we like to buy for our boys, and the sneakers aren't teaching them a &%$* thing.

I took them and still take them to cultural events; mostly African American, but not only African American. There is not a place we travel to, that I do not try and find the African American flavor of that area. We have gone to places like Boley, Oklahoma, where they have an annual All Black Rodeo. Let me tell you, you have not seen a rodeo until you have seen an all black one. After all, we were the original cowboys. We have gone to the gravesites of the Buffalo Soldiers. The Great Blacks in Wax Museum of Baltimore, Maryland, was a wonderful experience. The home of Benjamin Banneker was just amazing. We have been to the Dusable Museum of Chicago, and the Charles H. Wright Museum of Detroit, Michigan. Oh, I looks for my peoples.

You are probably saying I cannot afford to travel-not true. It just takes planning. I would not do it until they were old enough to remember anyway. But if you set aside an account while they are young, just put $10.00 a month in it, that's $120.00 a year. Don't touch it for 10 years—you do the math. By the time they are ten years old you will have enough to take them on a really nice trip. The problem is we do not have the discipline. However, we will buy that Yaki hair faithfully from those Koreans who are taking their children all over the world with our money.

I have introduced them to the arts. My children and I have performed in plays at one of our local African American theatres. Having been a dancer myself and performed before live audiences, my boys have been right there with me. My one son is musical and I've tried to take him to musical events of every kind. These events have usually been free.

We have also gone from the West, the Grand Canyon in Arizona, to the East, Plymouth Rock, in Plymouth, Massachusetts. We have gone camping in Indiana.

They have played organized sports, in the areas of baseball, basketball, football, and golf. They have taken swimming lessons. They then competed on the swim team of their elementary school. They have taken tennis lessons.

They have tried martial arts. They have taken chess lessons. They have competed in Chess tournaments and won. What is my point? Children of other ethnicities are not smarter, they are just exposed. Some of these lessons have been free. Some have cost, but the cost has never been unaffordable.

What does this exposure do for our children? For one, it gives them confidence. My boys are very competitive as most African American boys are. They need to use that competitive nature in some type of constructive way. They need to win at something. My boys were never on a winning team. However, they have had individual victories, which is even better. I have trophies in my home for baseball, football, basketball, and chess. Yes, even chess.

Television, video games and the internet are our worst enemies, because our children become slaves to them and do not use their brains or their creativity. However, many parents use these items to babysit their children while they do what they want to do. As I said in my introduction, being a parent is a lifestyle; it is not about us anymore, not on a large scale. It is about the children. If your children

Some Will Be King

are not in front of the TV, video games or the internet, that means you have to use your imagination and come up with an alternative. That is where going to freebies like an event at the zoo or museum would come in handy. In the summer, I would pack a lunch, we would jump on the bus or train and make it a day of adventure.

There are a lot of freebies out there, but you have to look for them. Remember, community center bulletin boards, bulletin boards at the library and the church are good sources for what is free in the city.

Exposure helps your children in school, teachers were amazed at how much my boys knew. Sometimes they were envious, because a lot of them have a problem when our African American boys appear to know a lot. It dispels the myth about our people and some individuals have a real problem with that. Something on the inside of them wanted to be the ones to expose my children. Because after all, these were just ghetto kids from the inner city.

Exposure gave my children a thirst for the unknown. They love to travel and do not have a fear of going anywhere, even without me. My boys went to a predominately-white Christian camp for a few summers. I was worried because it was far away from home. I did not worry too much about their safety when I let them go places, because they had each other. I was worried that they would not treat them right. However, in spite of a few incidents, my boys were able to overlook some name-calling and look at the bigger picture. The bigger picture was they got to go horseback riding every day and they loved it. They were able to go rock climbing. They were able to go swimming. They were able to ignore some ignorant children that were there, because my boys know who they are. No matter what you say to them, they do not internalize what outsiders say to them.

Exposure has opened my world up. I have met so many interesting people, because of my traveling with my children to different competitions and events. I have learned that other children are not smarter, just exposed. We have to expose them. We cannot depend on the school system, especially public. Public schools often do not have the time or the resources. Our children are no different than any other children. They have that thirst to learn. However, some of us as parents do not have that thirst to learn, so we do not value education or learning. You had it though parents; somehow, through life and life's circumstances it was taken away from you. For your children's sake; however, I sincerely beg you to make an effort to get it back. Find that thirst for learning again. It is a never-ending lifestyle. We do not know half of what we think we know. The more I learn the more I realize how much I do not know. I still look at life through childlike eyes full of wonder and curiosity. Remember, children of other ethnic backgrounds are not smarter, just exposed.

Each ethnic group has a uniqueness in how they learn and how they express what they have learned. That is the beauty of diversity. People are often amazed at how when an African American learns something, they start to dominate in that field. Like sports for example, when we start playing certain sports, the next thing you know we are dominating. However, sports are not the only fields where we dominate, if given a chance to enter. Science is based on facts, theories and discoveries. We also do well in the world of science, because in order for you to make a discovery you have to be a creative thinker. Creativity is our gift. We excel in the world of music and dance, again, because you have to be able to constantly come up with something new and appealing. Just look at all the styles of music there are and we were responsible for most of them. But, unfortunately, a lot of our children will never know how raw, as the youngsters say, they really are. Get your children up from in front of that television and take them somewhere they have never been before. I do not care if it is on the other side of town and you just walk up and down the street. Just expose them to something they have never seen or heard before.

Even if the experience is not a pleasant one, you may be treated rudely; however, make that a teachable moment on how to handle yourself in those situations. Let your children see that even though obstacles may come in their way, you still push forward if it is something that you want. That is why I would not let that nasty woman at the Science Museum deter us from coming. It also gave my children a sort of haughtiness when we went to these predominately white places. They would make me laugh sometimes because they would walk right up to anyone and say excuse me, I would like so and so and such and such. They have no fear of anyone, if it is something they want. My one son was sort of shy and could be intimidated once he asked, but

Some Will Be King

he would still ask. The other one could not be intimidated; he would look you right in the eye. I would turn my back sometimes, then turn around and see them engaged in conversation. I would go over to see what was happening and someone would be showing them something interesting and a lot of times the persons would be flattered that my children wanted to know. Again, other children are not smarter, just exposed.

Questions:

1. Why is exposure so important?
2. What were some of the things you were exposed to as child? Did it help in your development?
3. What, if any, organizations do you or child belong to.
4. Do you take your child to outside events; such as the theatre, zoo, or church?

Exercise:

Take your child to an event, then have them write about the event.

Chapter 5

I am not a father

This chapter is hard for me because it can be a volatile subject depending on whom you are talking to. I did not go to church today. It is June it's Father's Day. I didn't feel like hearing people tell me Happy Father's Day, because "I have been a mother and a father too." That statement turns my stomach. *I Can Never Be a Father.*

Single mothers, your boy needs a man in his life. There, I said it. They need a man for validation, approval, identity, and example. Do not get it twisted; not just any man will do. They need positive black male role models. Because, guess what, whether you provide one for them or not, they are going to find one. That is how young drug dealers are born. That is how young gang members are formed. Those boys were looking for identity. They were looking for approval, and they were looking for validation.

If you don't have any positive black men in your life, then you have to seek for them. Then the argument becomes whom do you want your child to be like? There is a disconnect in some of our neighborhoods, in some of our communities and I do not want to sound like I am trying to give middle class values to people who do not feel like they relate to these values. However, I just cannot believe that any mother, regardless of what neighborhood or income level, wants her child to become a criminal, or a ward of the state. So, that being said, I am going to continue this conversation as if all mothers want their boys to be successful.

Coaches are sometimes good influences. Most of the time if you have a black man, who is willing to sacrifice his time coaching other people's children, you have a decent black man. Tell him your situation. I have never closed the door on my boys' father as far as his being involved in their lives. I would never do that to my boys. He chooses not to get involved. Therefore, I had to seek other positive male role models. If you cannot find a black one, get whatever you can get as long as he is a positive influence.

One of the best influences for my boys was a ministry at our church, one of the few and one of the best, "Boys to Men." This ministry is wonderful in that it deals with developing the whole person. Now I realize that this is a rare program, and we are truly blessed. I recommend; however, that if you are not in a church home, seek one, and if you are a single mom raising a male child, shop for a church like you shop for anything else, if you're a shopper. Take your time.

Look for a church that has a strong youth ministry with qualified individuals running it. Ask the pastor what credentials the individuals working with the children have. They should have some background in working with children. If the pastor goes on the defense, walk away, because there is too much room for fraudulent activities in a lot of churches.

There is room for sexual abuse in some churches, because they have not set up guidelines. Ask if the people working with children have had police background checks. It is okay ... you can ask this. Do not lay your hands on anything quickly. These are the words of the Apostle Paul; they are so true. Wait, watch, observe and ask questions. If your instincts tell you that something is not right, then it probably is not. However, I was fortunate in that the men at my church were credible and supportive.

Some Will Be King

Again, on Father's Day it is very common for people to say to a single mom, "Happy Father's Day." I'd cringe whenever someone would say that to me, because I have been the world's greatest mother; I will never deny that, but I could never be a father. However, people with good intentions will say "You have had to be a mother and a father too." Again I say, not true. I have no clue what fatherhood is; I do not have the mind of a man. A father gives any child balance. A father gives the male perspective. I am not a man; I can only be a mother. I can only do my best to find substitute fathers because their father is not there.

Some Will Be King

Some Will Be King

I let the man, who has been in my life for some years know up front, if you want to be with me, it's a package deal. We had some rough times in the beginning. He did not have children and he was self-centered. He would compete with the boys for my attention. I told him I would make time for us, but do not ever get it twisted, I would never put him before my boys. I also broke it to him as gently as I could that there was no competition. I will never choose him over them, unless they were grown and on their own.

We joke about it now. He knows his place. It took a while for him to get it. I had to keep reminding him that I was a mother before I could be anything else. If it meant sacrificing our relationship, then that is what it meant. I noticed something about their relationship. No boy is going to like the man who is dating his mother, unless the man starts dating her when he is a baby. However, as much as they did not like him, there were times when they would reach out to him. They wanted his approval.

I was constantly bringing that to his attention. He most of the time missed it, because they would give him such a hard time. He wasn't in tune to what they needed. It got better, as they became older, but I can't help but think how it should have been. Now they cannot get enough of this man. They want him at every milestone in their lives. They truly love him. That is because he is a good person and over time they bonded. As I stated earlier in the book, boys will seek out a role model and as much as they fought against it, he showed them what commitment was.

My one son, I will refer to him as twin one, took music lessons from a seasoned citizen in our community who ran a music school. This man became a grandfather to my son. He was always presenting my son with opportunities to play music. Sometimes he would even pay him. My son eventually started playing drums for a small Baptist church. The pastor and his wife were long time friends of mine. This man also has a positive influence on my son. I am truly blessed.

I found men who were chess players in the community, because my other son, twin two, had a love for the chess game. Because of these men my son was very competitive in the community against children in his age group. He was the top player in the children's division. He became bored with playing with children in his age group and began playing just adults; he was quite competitive. These men were very supportive.

Boys need to talk to men about men's things. My boys went to a prayer breakfast for men one day. They went with a man. They needed to see men who are not afraid to worship God and know God and express it publicly.

If your boys do not have positive black role models, then don't stop them from having a white male mentor; it is still a man. You want a man who is capable of giving your son a positive influence. My boys have had white mentors as well as black. They had camp leaders who treated them very special. They had a history teacher who was a chess enthusiast who exposed them to chess tournaments. They had some coaches who were decent to them. So there, I said it, your boys need a man in their lives, and I am not taking it back. I am not a father.

Questions:

1. What are the attributes of a father versus a mother?
2. Did you have a father in your life? If not, how did that make you feel? If so, what do you appreciate about having him there?
3. Are there positive role models for your sons?

Some Will Be King

Exercise:

Talk to your sons about their father. Make a note of what they have to say. If your son does not have a father figure, make a plan on how to get one.

Chapter 6

We are not just body but we are also spirit

I do not know too many African Americans that do not have some type of spiritual base. However, there is becoming a whole generation that has no knowledge of God. This is a scary thought for those of us who have lived a little bit and know that there is definitely something or someone bigger than we are. I call him Jesus; there are others who call him Jehovah, some Allah, and then there are others that call him other things.

I do not want to harp on what you call him in as much as I want to focus on why we need him. We need a spiritual life because as you live and grow you come to know and understand that there are forces out there in life that we cannot see. However, we know that they exist. One of those forces is air; we do not see air but we know it exists. We do not see thoughts, but we know we have them. We do not see music, but we know it exists because we hear it. We do not see gravity, but nothing that goes up seems to stay up without help. We do not see emotions, but we know we have them because we feel them. We feel even though we do not see our feelings. We cannot see faith, but we have it. I know that my faith in God has been my anchor. It has been my stability.

As long as you are on this earth, you are going to seek answers. One of the biggest questions you are probably going to ask yourself one day, is why am I here? Some of the other questions you are probably going to ask are: What is my purpose in life? Why did this happen in my life? Why did that happen in my life? Why is this happening right now? Will this ever end? Why am I not happy after having everything I want? Why do I not have anything that I want? Why am I jealous? Why do I get so angry? I have the job that I want, but I am not happy. I am driving the car I want, but I still feel a void. I have the clothes I want, but I still feel inadequate. I live in the home that I wanted, but I still feel lonely at times. Why did my loved one have to die and leave me? Why didn't my father or mother love me? Why do people treat me wrong? How did I get so lucky, because I know I didn't deserve it? What happens when we die? Who has the answers? Who is telling the truth? How do they know? How can we trust? Where are the answers?

I believe the answers are inside of us, the part of us that we cannot see, the spirit man. What your boys become is going to be what they are fed. Because you see our spirit man, just like our physical man, has an appetite. One feeds off of actual food that you can taste and touch. The other feeds off of what we read, hear and see. He is spirit and he stays hungry, but not for anything that we can taste or touch in the natural. That is why material things will never satisfy him. (I talk about the spirit inside of us in a masculine form, but it applies to both male and female).

Organized religion can be a good source for this spiritual food. It is not the only source. It can be a great place of learning and growing, if the persons in charge are credible. There are many great institutions out there. Unfortunately, there is a lot of fraudulent stuff out there. I recommend people read the bible from cover to cover. When I say cover to cover, I mean cover to cover. Then I recommend that you study other spiritual books. You have to be careful not to get caught up in religion, and seek to have relationship with the creator. There is a voice inside of us which is God, the Almighty Counselor. That is where I get my strength and wisdom from. I do not take credit for anything that comes to my mind. Because I know that I did not create my mind. I do know that when I came into the knowledge of Him, my life became much more fulfilling, and had meaning. I also made better decisions about my life.

Help your boys find their spirit man. Because we have a spiritual life, my boys are calm when it counts. What does that mean? That means that they stay in control most of the time because they have a consciousness of God. They feel guilt, when they should. They have remorse for what they have done. They think positive thoughts and want to be involved in positive things, because they do not have an appetite for negative things. They think about the mysteries of life. They have compassion for the vulnerable and a heart for people.

Because of our beliefs and faith, they know where to seek the answers. I can only tell you what my experience has been. I cannot make you believe anything. However, if you have ever asked yourself those aforementioned, critical questions, just remember that the answers are inside of you; but the only way to pull them out is through the word of God. We are not just body, but we are also spirit.
Questions:

    1. Is spirituality a part of your life?

2. Are your children active in any type of spiritual activities?

3. What do you tell your children when they ask moral questions?

Exercise: Read a spiritual book.

Chapter 7

Hoorah!

African Americans are the most watched creatures on this earth. Because of this, they are constantly fighting; fighting for respect, fighting for their place, fighting for their rights, and fighting for their dignity. It is bittersweet, raising black boys. They are a joy, they are so smart, they love hard, and they play hard. But life for them is going to be hard. So we have to be their cheerleaders. You have to fight for them.

One of the many fights will be in some school systems with teachers ... teachers who are in it for the job, and summers off, because they do not have the gift or call. I'm sorry if I'm offending anyone, but the truth will set you free. As much as some of them want to do right, it is not in their heart, for the most part, in as much as it is their head. They mean well, but most white teachers do not understand us. They do not understand our energy. They do not understand how we interpret. Therefore, for me, it has been a battle. My boys for the most part, I will say 98%, are well behaved. It was confusing for me at times, because I would have some people telling me how well behaved and good they were, then I had others telling me they were a menace to society.

One of my boys, I will call him "the challenge," had a smart mouth, but he is brilliant. I found that most teachers would lose focus on how brilliant he is, and get caught up in his personality. I was supportive of the teachers; I wasn't one of those parents who wanted to fight the teacher. I let all teachers know, I am on your side. I would get in his behind about that mouth of his, and I was determined that I was not going to allow it to be a crutch for him.

You would think that would be half the battle in our parent-teacher relationship, but somehow he managed to get under their skin. They would take it personally, and start to resort to his behavior and then I would lose respect for them. I noticed that a black male child can have the same type of personality as a white male child and it is never seen as a threat.

However, whenever he had an African American teacher, the approach to him would be a little different. He loved his 5th grade teacher, Cheryl. She was African American, and she always seemed to be able to look beyond his personality and focus on his gifts. We would get in his stuff together, the teacher and I, when he was being difficult, and then tomorrow was a new day.

He loved those teachers and tried to be better in their classes. They never took his behavior personally. They looked at it as a challenge. The same thing would happen whenever they had a black coach, or Sunday school teacher. The approach to their personalities was just different. Whenever I would talk to a male of color about his personality, their approach was always different. It was never negative, even though they may be getting on their last nerve.

They never made me feel like I had the worst child on the earth. Most of them would tell me, "You have good children, do not worry. The one is a little flip at the lips, but we can handle him."

Do not get me wrong. They had some white teachers, who were wonderful. Thank you, Sheila. No matter what, she would always have something positive to say. The Music teacher at my son's elementary school, Teddy, was an angel sent from above, thank you. Cheryl, the Art teacher, was also a gem. Matt proved to be a friend, thank you.

One of the usual responses to our boys' high energy, was to try to put them in special education classes. My son, "the challenge", by the time he got to eighth grade, was taking ninth grade algebra and had a 100 average in the class. He also got accepted at almost every high school he applied for. However, he would have been in a special education class if I had listened to the one teacher. She was determined she was going to put him in a class for disruptive children.

Again, I do not condone my children being disruptive, but it was kind of hard for me to believe everything she was saying, by the simple fact, that when I showed up at the school to talk to her, she would be rude and inconsiderate. We were becoming hostile in our meetings, and finally I told the principal that I wanted to try him in another classroom.

I never commented on her rudeness toward me, because I didn't want it to become a pissing match. So, I just simply asked to change his classroom. For some strange reason they did not want to do it. I to this day believe that deep down inside they knew he would respond differently, because I was going to see to it, and they did not want to be wrong.

It just so happened, that this same teacher broke her ankle towards the middle of the school year. A black female teacher came in as a substitute. I was so shell shocked behind this other teacher, that when I came in to meet the substitute teacher for a conference, I had my head down, waiting for the ax to fall.

She was looking at me smiling; she told me that she had no problems with my son and that when he got a little out of hand, she just told him, "you don't want me to call your mother, do you?" and he would straighten right up.

My job was flexible. I could leave at any time. Therefore, he knew that I could show up at a moment's notice. She told me she enjoyed my son because he challenged her. She said he was very enthusiastic about learning. I wanted to cry ... I think I did.

I remember one teacher telling me that my son "the challenge" feels superior to most kids in the class. I remember kind of laughing to myself and thinking, I would rather he feel superior, rather than inferior. Neither one is good. But if I only had two choices, I know you can guess which one I'm picking.

My other son, I will call him "the creative one" was never really a threat to most teachers because he wasn't verbally difficult. He also did not have a lot of confidence in his academic abilities. I noticed, though, that they really didn't push him because they figured he was operating at his capacity. This would infuriate me.

They would allow him to slack off and not tell me about missing homework assignments or his not passing a test until it was almost too late. That was a different kind of battle; because, I knew he could do better. He was just not focused and didn't really care about academics. He's my creative one, and schoolwork just stood in the way of what he really wanted to be doing. Therefore, I had to really stay on top of him and push him to get good grades.

I was always reminding him that I knew it was an inconvenience to him to have to do his schoolwork, because he had more important things to do like play music or basketball, but he was just going to have to bear with us while we made him do his work. He was just as smart as his brother; he just did not care. However, he also tested very well and was accepted at most of the high schools he applied for. He is a left-brain thinker and he draws conclusions in a different manner.

When my son "the challenge" got close to going to high school, I found a program that prepares minorities for private schools and helps them obtain scholarships. This program groomed him and pushed him academically, and emotionally. They pushed these children hard because the private schools in our area were predominately white, and not real receptive to minority students.

Someone had studied the success rate of minority students in these schools, and decided that they wanted to help change the numbers. They realized that this depended on some grooming for these children ahead of time.

My son "the challenge," upon completing the program, had a made-up mind and looked forward to going to a school that he felt would be challenging, but would give him a superior education. It was an all boys school. He was the only black child in most of his classes. He focused on his studies and did not let it shake him that he was the only one in his class. He also was not afraid to speak up or out about something he felt strongly about. His teachers were amazed with him and found him to be a pleasure in class.

He was a 9th grader; however, he was taking 10th grade math and science and was on the Honor roll. This was the boy that the fourth grade teacher wanted to put in special education classes. Imagine if I had listened to her. It has not been an easy experience for him.

I will never forget his first day of school. I felt so sorry for him. He was like a fish out of water. There were no boys there from his old school. The boys he knew there were upperclassmen. He did not see them until it was time to get on the bus. He had to feel isolated. It is one thing to be the new kid at school. However, he was the only black new kid at school, in most of his classes and some of the white kids did not make him feel better.

The year he started at the school was the President Obama election year. The atmosphere was charged everywhere and race was the focus of most discussions. He would be sitting in class and some of the boys would gang up on him about President Obama. He would be so upset some days when he came home. I reminded him that he chose to go to that school knowing the obstacles that he would have to face. and asked now what did he want to do? He decided he wanted to stay. I'll never forget how he felt the day President Obama won. It was a victory for him as an African American boy facing his own odds.

We had another setback at the school. He tried out for the freshman varsity basketball team. My son "the challenge" is not a super star basketball player; in fact, sports is not his strength. He can play, he has the desire, but the skill level is just not there. However, he wanted to play because he still had dreams of being a great player.

He made the team. The coach was a volunteer parent coach. He and my son did not see eye to eye the first week. My son knew the man did not like him and he did not make the situation any better. So one day, the coach exploded on him and asked him, and I quote, "Who in the %#ck do you think you are?"

I called the principal, the president, and the athletic director. They all gave me superficial sympathy and promised me that nothing like that would ever happen again. I knew they were full of baloney and I lost respect for all of them after that. I asked my son did he still want to play. He tried to continue, the coach never said anything harsh to him again; however, he would purposely not put him in the game. So my son eventually quit.

Ordinarily, I would never let my children quit something just because it was not easy. However, there was nothing to gain with staying on this team. In fact, it was stripping his self-esteem; we had already gone through something like this before and I learned from that never to allow my children to stay in something that was taking away from them, instead of giving them something. However, even going through this he still was able to focus on his studies and get good grades.

I thought we were home free until the very last week of school, when the school disciplinarian called me to tell me that "the challenge" had an incident on the public bus with some girls from another private school, which precipitated them putting him on disciplinary probation. For the first semester of his sophomore year, he was to be on probation.

When he came back in September, he was walking around on eggshells because if he sneezed wrong they were going after him. I, along with his father, who I begged to go with me, went to the school to talk to whoever would talk to us, because we simply were not having it. I kindly asked them while they were so busy watching "the challenge," who was paying attention to the other children? They looked a little dumbfounded, and my son did not seem to have any more problems after that.

My son "the creative one,'" after much contemplation on my part, as well as his, decided to go to a public high school. The high school was one of the best high schools in the inner city. It was not a high school for underachievers, it actually was the opposite—a school for high achievers. You had to test to get in the school and it was highly competitive. It had many programs, which the other high schools did not have and was always getting recognition.

He loved the school the first day. I knew it would fit his personality and he had friends there from his old school, so he felt no isolation. I thought we were home free. Until my son who, mind you, was a 9th grader taking 10th grade math and science like his twin brother, got his first report. He was failing chemistry, 10th grade science. Did I tell you that he was just a 9th grader?

Well like any concerned parent who was ready and willing to do whatever it took to help my child get through this, I came in to talk to the teacher. It was parent-teacher conference night. The teacher was rude, condescending, and nasty. I was livid when I left school that night. His other teachers were nice and professional and gave me the impression they cared.

I wrote a letter to the principal, because I decided to start a paper trail. So, the second time I came back, this same teacher's whole demeanor had changed; however, there was still a pinch of arrogance there; he could not hide it.

The principal was in a dilemma. He knew I was telling him the truth; however he felt peer pressure to protect his teacher. I would not let him off the hook. I told him I wanted my son out of that teacher's class. He took him out. My son did not have to take that class until he was a senior; therefore, there was no need for him to take it as a freshman.

In the meantime, it was preventing him from playing basketball, because you could not play basketball if you were not passing a class. He was not going to pass this class, because they did nothing to try to assist in that happening. I came in and I asked for the curriculum. I asked to see his test. I asked about tutoring, which they claimed they had.

I got no cooperation. It was a joke. They knew it; because when I exposed them, they had no choice but to take him out. They could sense that I was going to be a pain in the neck to them. I call my son the underachiever, but when I put fire under his butt, he does what he has to do. I would have put fire under his butt about this class, had the teacher given me direction on how to help him. However, the teacher did everything in his power to fail him. I would not let him give him a failing grade.

However, the teacher still won, because my son was removed from class, which is what he wanted. They won the battle with that one; however, they did not win the war. What they did not know was that I was not finished with them. I had just retreated long enough to strategize how I was going to deal with them.

Some of the teachers tried to demonize my son; however, it is kind of difficult to demonize a child who is respectful, low key and does not cause problems. The English teacher accused him of cheating on his test one day so I came in. I asked to talk to the teacher, along with my son, because after all, everyone is entitled to face his or her accuser. The teacher would not talk to us. The principal would not make him. I started a paper trail on that teacher.

My son was able to play basketball; however, the coach let him know in no uncertain terms that he was not as good as he thought he was and he better get better grades in his classes.My son was as good as he thought he was, because unlike his brother, he was a very talented athlete.

In fact, he was so good, that the coach put him on a special tournament team. That was ironic to me. He tells him he's not as good as he thinks he is; however, he picks him to play on a special tournament team. Which one is it? Either he's good or he's not. I can understand you not wanting a kid to become too cocky. Then don't put him on the team; tell him to try again next year.

My son had three more years to play basketball. Little did this coach know, I couldn't care less if my son played basketball; my concern is always going to be about his academics. But as always, they stereotype us, that all we care about is sports. However, I did care about the attitudes of the teachers and coaches. I did not like their techniques.

Reports by the American Council on Education, the Education Trust and the Schott Foundation show that African American boys spend more time in special education, spend less time in advance placement or college prep courses and receive more disciplinary suspensions and expulsions than any other group in U.S. schools today. The Schott Foundation started the Black Boys initiative in 2003, says President Rosa Smith, because "black boys represented the worst-case scenario for a group coming out of public education."

After my son, the "creative one's" first year in high school, I was hoping that things would mellow out. Things did just the opposite. Every time I turned around, he was being expelled from school for something. The school security guard did not like him and he was determined he was going to get him kicked out of the school and off the basketball team. Well he did manage to get him kicked off the team that year. However, I was determined that he was not getting kicked out of school.

Not only was the security guard after him, unfortunately, there was an African American assistant principal who saw black boys as a menace as well and she too tried to get him kicked out. I fought her, though, and I fought the system and I did it with intelligence and I would not let them wear me down.

I never went into the school to talk with administrators by myself. I always had advocates go with me. I would beg their father to go in with me. You have to let them know that your children have people in their lives who are going to fight for them. If not, they will treat them like a stereotypical ghetto child with no father and a crack head mother.

In the "creative one's" third year, he managed to get through without any problems, no suspensions. He got along with all of his teachers, except one. The basketball coach asked him to come back and play basketball—they had a love-hate relationship.

I dismissed myself from the whole basketball thing altogether, because I was tired of them dangling basketball in front of us like a carrot all the time. I wanted my son to concentrate on his grades. He did only what it took to pass, nothing more nothing less. We made it to his last year of high school; he was on the basketball team and local college coaches started recruiting him for college. But he still had one teacher, the one from the previous year, who he just did not get along with.

Both of my boys worked all summer, forty hours a week. They worked so well for the owner that he told both of them that they had jobs for life with him. During the school year, they worked for him after school. The "creative one" was either at work or basketball practice during the week after school. On the weekends he would socialize with a certain group of kids that I knew. They were good kids.

On Sundays he was in church just about all day, because he played drums and was still loyal to that. I had never smelled drugs on him or his brother. Neither one of them had bedrooms that I could not get into. They never even smelled like alcohol. My boys just did not have the desire.

So you can imagine my shock and disappointment when I got a call from the school that the "creative one" was being suspended for possession of marijuana. I was devastated. But as the story unfolded it proved to be more of a suspicion than believable. According to the teacher that the "creative one" did not get along with, this teacher asked my son for his hall pass. When my son reached in his pocket he saw something fall out. He and my son walked back into the classroom together to look at the clock. He let my son go to his session that he was supposed to be going to.

My son walked up the hallway, and this teacher called him back and said he found a baggy of marijuana on the floor and he believed it belonged to my son, and that was what must have fallen out of his pocket. The principal, who was new, suspended my son and we had to go before one of the school superintendents to find out what they were going to do with him.

That night I went to the drug store and bought a marijuana testing kit. I made my son take it. He tested negative for marijuana. I was not surprised and very relieved. He had no signs of selling drugs. No large sums of money hidden in his room. No clothes that I did not know how or when he bought them. No drugs in his room. No change in his behavior, nothing that indicated drug use or sales. So, I believed my son and I was locked and loaded for battle. I also prayed and depended on God to work this out for us.

I went to the school the next morning with his father and his godfather. We fought for him and let the principal know that we were not going to take this teacher's word for it. They claimed they had it on film, but they refused to show us the film. The meeting ended. We waited for the hearing, which would be held by a school board representative in our city hall. In the meantime, my son was suspended, missing classes and kicked off the basketball team temporarily. His future as far as college was looking fragile.

I felt good about the upcoming hearing for several reasons. One reason was that I felt we had a strong enough argument to cast reasonable doubt. I also felt there was some fabrication going on and as long as we stuck to our guns and the truth, I felt justice would be done.

"The creative one's" boss, who was an attorney, said he would give us representation on that day. However, we wound up not even needing it. On the day of the hearing, myself, and "the creative one's" father showed up to the hearing together. We were well dressed, neat and on time.

The principal came with the teacher, and the security guard who had written a statement. We went into the hearing; we presented ourselves in a civilized manner. We were cool, but humble, so much so, that the principal felt bad; I could tell by his demeanor. When we left the hearing, my son, his father and I proceeded up the hallway to the elevators of the building. I happened to turn around and look behind me. I saw the principal go back into the hearing officer's office. I believe he went back in to speak on the "creative one's" behalf.

We had to wait another week for the hearing disposition. The "creative one was found not guilty due to the accuser's testimony, which could not substantiate the charges. The charges were to be removed from his school records and he was placed back on the basketball team. This was a hard lesson for my son. It humbled him, and he realized that these people did not have his best interest at heart and he better smarten up and watch his back. I kept trying to tell him "you are in the real world now, buddy and the real world does not like you."

Fortunately for me but unfortunate for a disturbing number of parents, while my two boys graduated from high school, some students who have no support, get discouraged and quit school, serve time in jail or worse.

The high schools my sons attended won some battles; but, we won the war. The "challenge" graduated from the University of Pittsburg Cum Laud; this was the one the teacher wanted to put in special education. The other one graduated from Erie Community College and as of this writing is a Junior at Buffalo State College.

Nel Noddings, a professor at Stanford University, a former K-12 math teacher and the author of several books on caring, observed that "young black men and boys growing up without male role models and in conditions of poverty probably do need, more than anyone else, that assurance that somebody really cares."

In an article from the Washington Post, August 2005, Daniel de Vise, <u>Special-Ed Racial Imbalance spurs sanctions,</u> two Maryland school systems were among five that faced state sanctions because they were steering too many struggling black students into special education with problems that, in a number of cases could be addressed in a regular classroom, according to federal education officials. The school system had to spend a combined $8 million a year on efforts to reduce the number of black students in special-ed.

Harvard University put out a book in 2002 titled "The civil rights project at Harvard University." In this book the subject of inequities experienced by minority school children in special education and the potential life consequences of such inequities was explored. The book also covers, the overrepresentation of minority children in special education.

In December 1999, the Education Law Reporter stated that black students are being expelled at rates two to three times higher than white students and receiving more severe punishment than their white counterparts for the same infractions. The research dispels a simplistic explanation of a disproportionate level of misbehavior by minority students but rather points to a biased system where a double standard appears to exist.

Civic Report No.48, April 2006, from the Manhattan Institute for Policy research calculated the graduation rates of public high school students by race and gender. The results were: The national overall graduation rate was about 70 percent. At only 48 percent, African American male students reported the lowest graduation rates of any subgroup nationally, compared to 65 percent for white males. We have to be involved, get involved and stay on top of our boys because we cannot expect the school system or anyone else to care about them. It is a sad reality, but a reality nonetheless. An author that I recommend you also read is one by the name of Dr. Jawanza Kunjufu. He has several books on this subject, excellent reads.

Do not let teachers or principals intimidate you when you go in to talk about your children. They will try to do it. If you feel like you need an advocate to talk for you, then find one and use them. You do not have to talk to them alone. Do not talk to them alone if you cannot express yourself and feel insecure. Go to the school board and lodge a complaint. Let them know that you will go to the school superintendent.

I put my boys on an organized little league baseball team. It was a predominately-white league. I chose this league simply because, and I hate to say it, but they were organized. The black little league baseball team at the time was very much unorganized and poorly supported. It was too time consuming to try and deal with them. Therefore, I put them in this predominately white league.

They were never treated fairly or right. I kept leaving it up to them each year to decide if they wanted to go back. They always wanted to go back. Each year as they got older it seemed to get worse. I would leave that park some days so angry; ready to come back with a semi-automatic, and do a drive by, but instead I had to just pray. There was never a good season, until they had a Puerto Rican coach.

This coach treated them fairly and he did not care what other parents or the league officials said or thought. His wife was wonderful also. The league was a good and bad experience. The good was just like Jackie Robinson, my boys had to have a lot of heart and strength to endure what they were enduring sometimes. It was somehow preparing them for real life.

The bad, they had to endure some bad treatment, and learn early that this world did not have their best interest at heart. I still to this day regret that I allowed them to be subjected to the treatment they received from the league. However, not having that man there to give me support or advice, I did not make a good decision. Whenever they had to do something though, I was right there, telling them how wonderful they were, that they could do it.

Some Will Be King

I was honest with them; I told them when they were not doing so well. Then I would speak life back into them. Somehow they would get the strength to go on. We have been through a lot together. My children know that I will fight for them. They are funny though, because they will say to me sometimes, "Mom, calm down; it's not that serious." Then I know that they are all right. We have to be their cheerleaders, because believe me, no one else is going to be.

So here I am, telling people how wonderful they are. Telling the boys how wonderful they are. That in spite of how the world is treating them, they can make it. HOORAH!

Questions:

1. What challenges did you have to face with your sons?
2. Do you have an advocate for your son?
3. Are you involved with your children's school?
4. Has your child been suspended from school? If so, how did you handle it.

Some Will Be King

Exercise:

Meet with your child's principal and find out the policies that are in place to protect your child.

Chapter 8

Grasshopper

There was a martial arts movie that came out in the eighties, called the Karate Kid. We loved that movie. There was an old guy in the movie who was mentoring a young boy who wanted to learn karate. There was also a television show that came on called Kung Fu. The guy was a martial artist who also was mentored by an old teacher. That is a special relationship, the mentor and the mentee. Mentors usually do not have selfish motives; they want to see their mentee grow and go somewhere. They want to see their protégé go perhaps where they may have never gone or may not ever go, but they don't mind. In the Kung Fu series Master Po calls his young student "Grasshopper."

Once you discover your child's gift, find a mentor for them. I find that you usually do not have to look too far. When the student is ready the teacher will appear. Just putting your children in the right programs will precipitate the mentor finding them. My son "the creative one's" love for his music always drew people to him that wanted to help him.

As I stated earlier his elementary school music teacher, Teddy was probably one of his biggest influences. The "creative one" could do no wrong in her eyesight. Therefore, because she treated him like that, he was so motivated to participate in anything musical and he has a lot of confidence. One of my proudest moments was when he carried the baseline in the orchestra pit at a school play, playing the cello bass for an Italian opera. He showed true musicianship

The main drummer for the church we attend, gave the "creative one" some of his first drum lessons. He would allow the "creative one" to sit where the musicians sat. He

played drums for the children's choir at this same church before hundreds of people. He was a champion. He also participated in a music project a couple of summers called the Dunbar project, given by the local theatre group.

One of the teachers from this project, Rodney, an established musician in our city took "creative one" under his wing, and mentored his cello base and base guitar capabilities. If you expose your children, as I said before, mentors will emerge. As I stated earlier in the book, he had another music teacher, the late Mr. Martin "Pappy," who was not only a mentor but also a grandfather. He had him performing in parades and jazz concerts. He was a very positive influence in "creative one's" life.

Some Will Be King

My son, 'the challenge' is an introvert, and complex. It was hard trying to find his gift, because it wasn't something transparent like music or sports. He wasn't really good at sports, he was okay. He wasn't musical or into creative arts. His brother was always in the limelight and I wanted him to have something that gave him his own identity.

Unfortunately, in this world the emphasis is always on the athlete, or entertainer. I could tell it bothered him. He came home from summer camp one year, with this love for the game of chess. Whenever someone would come to our house, he would ask him or her if they could play.

However, I knew no one personally who played the game; I could not find an outlet right away in the community.

He joined the chess team at his elementary school and his homeroom teacher started to mentor him. Matt then introduced us to a chess tournament, and the doors came open for us to another whole world. We met some wonderful people. I then found some African American players at the community center around the corner from our house. It was there that I found a chess teacher for him. There was a guy, who at one time was one of the top players in the city.

Some Will Be King

He was what you would call a Master chess player. The guy wasn't doing too well when we met him; he was on a downward spiral mentally, brilliant individual, but something was missing. However, he still knew the game quite well. So in spite of his strange behavior at times, and some reassurance from some sane brothers I trusted, I felt secure that he would not hurt us. I let him mentor my son at chess.

We would meet him at a local coffee house. The "the challenge" won several chess tournaments at the local level. This gave him confidence, and I believe it was the turnaround for him, with his challenging behavior. Because he was such a mental person, chess was the mental challenge he needed. Coming home with a few trophies and one time some money can definitely be an ego booster. There is something about beating someone mentally at a game. We have chess books in our house and all kinds of chess sets. One of my proudest moments was when he played against the son of a chess grandmaster and almost beat him.

I then got him into another academic program and he became this highly motivated kid who wanted to do well academically and was proud to be smart. Those are just two examples of how mentors have helped my boys in their gifts.

Expose your children to different things; this leads to discovering their gifts. Once you discover the gift, nurture it. While you are nurturing the gift, find a mentor. The mentor will help make them into grasshopper

Some Will Be King

Questions:
1. What are your son's gifts or talents?
2. Is he currently involved in activity related to that gift?
3. What has your son shown an interest in?

Exercise: Find a mentor for your son's gift or talent.

Chapter 9

Those is some bad &^% kids

Some of us in the community have this mindset. We do not like anyone disciplining our children. There is also this thing when they are babies, that when they are acting out we think it is cute. Well guess what, you are the only one who thinks it is cute. Everyone else is rolling their eyes up in their head, wishing you would take those devil children somewhere else. It is highly, highly annoying. No one wants to be bothered with bratty kids.

It is not the child's fault; there is no such thing as bad children, just bad parenting. Children need discipline. They need to be corrected. If they did not, then they would come into this world as adults. Discipline is not about yelling all the time. It is not about hitting your children. I am old school; I do not see a problem with a little smack on the bottom every now and then to get their attention. However, you should not always have to respond in a violent manner to change your children's behavior. You will find that after a while they will stop responding to it anyway.

Discipline is teaching. Discipline is setting boundaries. Children need order and boundaries. You are the adult. You have to set the boundaries, and the order. Children do not know how to set boundaries. They have to be taught. However, if there is always chaos and confusion in your home because of a lack of stability, your children are going to act out.

If your children do not get enough attention, because perhaps you are working all the time, they are going to act out. If your children do not have something that brings them joy in their lives they are going to act out.

When children are tired because they do not have a consistent bedtime, they are going to act out. If they are hungry, they are going to act out. I hold on to the philosophy, that there are no bad kids, just bad parenting. You can't start setting the boundaries when they are teenagers. It is too late by then. Just think of how hard it is for you to stop doing something that you have been doing for the last ten or fifteen years. Behavior becomes a habit.

Habits are hard to break, because they become second nature.

So now you have this child entering into the world with certain bad habits. Habits like those listed below:

1. Talking all the time, and at inappropriate times. The old folks say "there's a time and place for everything." That is so true. Sometimes you need to just be quiet. Teach your children how to sit and be quiet sometimes. Have quiet time in your house. I used to make my children go to their room and no talking. I explained to them that there are times when you need to be quiet. Relax, think before you speak.

I realized when my son was talking a lot, that somehow he needed attention. So I would sit him down and ask, what is on your mind, because you are running off at the mouth way too much. Work on little projects with your children when they are small, that require concentration, so they will learn how to stay focused on something. Color with them in a coloring book. Draw with them. Have them cut out shapes.

Give them something to do besides television. Have them help you do something around the house that they can handle, even if they are doing it sloppy. Teach them how to be self engaged. I have had friends over my house ask me where are your boys? I would say in their room. They would be shocked because they were so quiet. My one son, "the challenge," would be in the house for hours and he was so quiet that I would forget he was home. They still are calm; even when they have friends over they are usually calm, unless they are arguing with each other. They are normal kids after all.

2. Talking back to adults is not cute. It is disrespectful. You are doing your child a disservice when you allow them to butt into conversations with adults, and when you allow them to be sarcastic with adults. You are doing them a disservice, because people will avoid them. No one wants to be rejected. Often they are the ones who get rejected, because they are annoying. People are not going to let you spoil their day, if they have a choice.

3. Fighting and being disruptive is not cute. Maybe you are disruptive, and you do not care. Do you notice that people look at you like you are crazy? It is because everyone has the right to a certain amount of common courtesy in public places. We are not on this earth by

ourselves. We do not have the right to infringe our noise and violent behavior on others. It is called harassment, and there are laws that prohibit this type of behavior. It is uncivilized.

Now you can do whatever you want in the privacy of your own home. No one is going to be upset with you. You can run through the house screaming to the top of your lungs buck-naked. However when you come out in public, it is just not fair or nice to infringe rude behavior on others. In school especially, teachers ignore rude children, or try to get rid of them.

My children were always engaged in some type of school activity or afterschool activity when they were in elementary school. I also was involved in the parent-teacher association. Children like us to be engaged. I'm telling you, I know that because of my involvement with their school. Somehow my children did not get into trouble. They were never suspended once over the ten years that they attended that school. One was suspended off the bus for fighting on the school bus. He just got tired of being bullied by a kid who was being allowed to terrorize the whole bus.

Some Will Be King

My boys were on the swim team, the chess team and the basketball team. My one son was like the lead musician whenever they had a program. I remember riding to our state capital with my son on the bus with the string orchestra. The school had played a little concert along with children from other schools, at the state capital building. My son played the cello bass for the string orchestra. The teacher for the string orchestra also informed me of a summer music project one year and she wanted my son to be involved. Also for about four summers in a row, my son was always bringing that huge cello home for the summer.

My boys learned early that if you are not disruptive and you are polite, good things come to you. People are always inviting them to something, *always*. Their social calendar is busier than mine. As a young adult my one son works at a public building doing building maintenance. There are several hundred employees in the building. He is the favorite of everyone, especially the ladies. One of the things that they all say to me is your son is so polite. They get free tickets to events, they get fed, and any other amenities they can drop on them they get.

Some Will Be King

We have to set boundaries; we have to have order in our home. Make sure they have a set bedtime and stick with it. Make sure they eat before they go somewhere. Teach them how to be self-engaged in quiet activity. You have to teach them how to do this though. That is hard to do when you are in front of the TV all the time, or talking on the telephone. This is not anything new and improved, just the basics. I guarantee you that if you start early and keep it up until they are teenagers, you will never overhear someone say about your children, "those is some bad &^% kids."

Questions:

1. What boundaries have you set up for your son?
2. If school age, do they have a specific bedtime?
3. Do you discipline your child?
4. How much time do you spend with your child?

Exercise: Spend some time with your child at home doing a project that requires concentration.

Chapter 10

Ignorance of the law is no excuse

I have worked for the criminal justice system for over thirty years, and one day it hit me. I had never really sat down and had a frank talk with my boys about the criminal justice system. They are likely to have an encounter with the law at one time in life. Our day came. I expected it at some point; however, knowing it's coming does not take the sting away, especially when you know that it was based on profiling.

The law is disproportionate, as far as contact, incarceration and representation are concerned, when it comes to African Americans. However most of us are ignorant as to what our rights are and how to behave in certain situations. I asked them both individually one day what would you do if you got arrested; what are your rights?

One did not know what he would do or his rights. The other one knew a little and kind of muddled through the rest. They thought I was being over the top of course, as they always think, because at their age, they felt invincible and did not take life that seriously. I did not want to take their childhood from them; they were only 15 years old. However they looked like men.

One is 6'4" and the other one is 5'9'. They did not understand that the police no longer saw them as little boys, but juvenile delinquents. They are going to be profiled, stereotyped, and discriminated against.

As in the case when my son had an incident on the bus, he and another African American boy, against some white females. Apparently there has always been trouble on this bus between these girls from another private school and African American boys on this bus. Mainly because the girls knew that the bus driver, along with the people on the bus, were going to come to their side. My son, again, went to a predominately white all boys private school. The bus that he rode on was going to a suburb.

Some Will Be King

I don't think I have to tell you the ending to the story. The bus driver sent a complaint to the school. The school disciplinarian called me after he had talked to my son and gotten a confession out of him. I was livid and I saw that my son was easily intimidated. They never wanted me to come in and talk to them about my son; they always wanted to talk to him alone. I know the game and it is going to continue all their lives, especially in certain areas.

An excellent book to read and have in your library is a book called *Fighting for Your Life: The African-American CriminalJustice Survival Guide* by John V. Elmore, Esq. I made my boys read it because ignorance of the law is no excuse.

One day I was celebrating my promotion to Asst. Deputy Superintendent with some friends. We had all met at a restaurant and had a good time. Afterwards I was over a girlfriend's house catching up on things in each other's lives and lost track of time because I wasn't under any time constraints. My girlfriend's doorbell rang; it was my one son the creative one and he was frantic because his brother was sitting in a jail cell at one of the suburban precincts, a precinct known for profiling African Americans. This is the jail where they arrested DMX and would not let him out on bail.

They had been calling me, but I did not have my cell phone on me. This was the last thing I was expecting to hear, because when I last talked to my boys they were going to a high school football game in this suburb. I told them before they went that I did not feel comfortable with them going to this game because neither one of them attended any of the schools that were playing. They were insistent about going. I realized that I had to let them go and just trust that they would make good decisions. I could not hold their hands forever. Therefore, I never gave them another thought, because the mother of one of the boys they were going with, was picking them up from the game. I knew her; she was a responsible parent.

Therefore you can imagine my shock when my creative son came to my girlfriend's door, stating they had been looking for me for a couple of hours. Well as the story goes my two boys; I will call one "street smart," and the other one I will call "book smart" were at the game as they said and a fight broke out between one of their friends and another kid from another school and neighborhood.

In the meantime the kid who was fighting who was with my boys, his mother was waiting for them in the parking lot of the school not realizing that her son was in a fight. Another boy attempted to jump in the fight, but my "street smart" kid jumped in it, got a few punches in and jumped out, because he realized the police had been called. He ran toward the parking lot to their friend's mother's car explaining to her what was happening.

My "book smart" son who wears glasses, but did not have them on, could not find the others because it was dark and a big cluster of kids was running everywhere. When he finally realized what was happening, the police were putting him in the back of a squad car, with his friend who was fighting. When they got to the precinct, the police were ready to let them go, but they would only release my son to a parent. So they had to find me; my boys did not trust their father enough to call him unfortunately. They gave my son a hearing date even though the other boys told the police that he was not involved in the fight.

I called their father and he agreed to come to the hearing with us. So there we were at the hearing and my son had on his private school uniform, looking non threatening and presentable. He had two parents with him on either side of him. He had no record and the judge wanted to know if we had an attorney. We said to him, "Your honor, why does he need an attorney when, first of all, it was kids fighting at a football game and no one got hurt? Second, my son was not one of the fighters." The judge said to us, "You either get a lawyer or your son could be facing up to a year in jail."

I could not believe what I was hearing. However, I was not surprised based on this suburb's reputation. It was one thing to hear about it, it was another thing to experience it. They contacted my son's private school, who in turn called me to let me know that they were waiting for the disposition on this hearing to decide if they were going to let him remain at the school; after all their school had a reputation to uphold. God forbid, you have two football game fighters at your school. That is just appalling. It took everything in me not to tell them what they could do with their school and their reputation.

I was livid! Livid with everyone white, the police, my son for being so stupid, myself for not knowing enough about the law and God for letting this happen. After I got over my anger I called my village: a god-brother who had a lot of knowledge in this area, but was not reliable. He explained what would be the outcome, and it would cost me to get a lawyer. I was living from paycheck to paycheck and I did not have money in my budget for that. I made too much money to get a court appointed attorney. I never trusted them anyway.

I called my pastor, who is highly connected and I had never called on him before for anything. He was more than happy to help me. He obtained a lawyer for us, who was a member of the church and he told me not to worry about the cost. This again supports my belief in belonging to a congregation that is community minded. The reality is our boys are more than likely to be arrested for something that a white boy would be released for as soon as his parents come to pick him up.

How the story ended was that my son was not to come into that suburb for six months, after which all charges would be dropped. The sad reality is my son had a village behind him and a momma who would never give up the fight. I can't help but feel for the boys who do not have that; it makes me shudder, because I know how they are railroaded in this system, which is why we need more of us in the system to make sure that this is not happening.

Questions:

1. What do you know about the criminal justice system and how it works?
2. What does your son know about the criminal justice system?
3. Do you know your rights if arrested?

Exercise: Read a book on the criminal justice system. Talk to your son about it.

Conclusion

I want to end this book talking about how we can never get enough hugs and affection. Healthy affection is definitely a cure for most things that are wrong with us. I am always kissing and hugging my boys. Now that they are young adults, they do not require it as much. I require it though and I want my hugs and kisses. My mother was very affectionate and I know that is why I'm so loving towards most people. Healthy affection has no sexual connotations. Your child is not your sex partner. When I talk about affection I am only talking about nonsexual.

Most social scientists, behaviorists, psychologists, psychiatrists, and people who study human behavior will tell you, (that is if they are healthy), that human beings need touch. My male friend used to always tease me about my one son being a mamma's boy. He was always up under me and I was always showing him a lot of affection. The thing he criticized me about with my son was the thing my friend was always craving, affection. He could not get enough. I always felt like I was dealing with a wounded puppy with him. His father did not allow him and his brothers to hang on to their mother. My one son who was always under me, is never under me at all, now; he hardly ever wants to hug or kiss me. I guess he got enough to sustain him.

Remember, every child is different and requires different things. The other boy always acted as if nothing bothered him. I knew he needed affection also, so I would hug and kiss him anyway, even though he pretended that he did not need it. He is very affectionate now. Tell those boys you love them. I guarantee you that if you do, you will be releasing Kings out into the world and not Killers. This is my story and this is my quest of being a King Maker.

Some Will Be King

The End

About the Author

Deborah Watkins is a retired Deputy Superintendent of Program Services for the New York State Department of Corrections and Community Supervision, and has worked in the field for over thirty years. She wore a few hats with the department starting as a prison guard. She did that for two and half years, leaving the stick and the uniform to become a civilian. As a civilian, she served as an ombudsman for the inmates, in a position called Inmate Grievance Supervisor for four and a half years. Because of her educational background and the desire to do something different again, she was able to switch over to the area of guidance and counseling and became a counselor. It was with guidance she discovered her gift for motivating people who have no hope, as a Corrections Counselor. After a number of years, she then became the supervisor over the unit. Later on she became the first female executive team member at the military boot camp prison known as Shock incarceration. Even though Corrections is viewed in a negative way, it was a rewarding career for her.

"The Department of Corrections, like most organizations, conducts periodic in house training. It was through this area that I discovered my gift and love for instructing. I became a Master trainer for the Department of

Some Will Be King

Corrections, in the area of cultural diversity, and other topics. This involved helping conduct train the trainer sessions for the department. Taking advantage of opportunities is the route I took in corrections. Helping to empower black people is my passion." Deborah holds a Master's degree in Organizational Leadership and a Bachelor's degree in Business Management. She is very involved with her community as a volunteer.

Printed in the United States
By Ingram Spark

www.ingramcontent.com/pod-product-compliance
Lightning Source LLC
Chambersburg PA
CBHW072045290426
44110CB00014B/1575